# THE MIND OF
# SWAMI VIVEKANANDA

THE MIND OF

# Swami
# VIVEKANANDA

An anthology and a study
by
**Gautam Sen**

# JAICO PUBLISHING HOUSE

Ahmedabad  Bangalore  Bhopal  Chennai
Delhi  Hyderabad  Kolkata  Mumbai

Published by Jaico Publishing House
121 Mahatma Gandhi Road
Mumbai - 400 001
jaicopub@vsnl.com
www.jaicobooks.com

© Gautam Sen

THE MIND OF SWAMI VIVEKANANDA
ISBN 81-7224-212-3

First Jaico Impression: 1975
Twentieth Jaico Impression: 2008

Printed by
New Radharaman Printers
20, Wadala Udyog Bhavan
Wadala, Mumbai-400 031

# CONTENTS

# Introductory Commentary

IT IS A matter of common observation that after a person dies, the image that lives on in the minds of his associates often does not tally with reality. With the passage of time a few additions, ommissions and embellishments solidify into such a shape as to transform the original person into quite another character. Hence, it is not surprising that the accounts of the lives and teachings of the founders and other leading figures of various religions should have undergone the same process.

Thus, by the time the ancient religious texts of India and the stories of the Ramayana and Mahabharata were actually written down, they were very different from their original versions. For example, the battle of Kurukshetra is described in the Mahabharata as an earth-shaking struggle in which practically every king in India participated; but a study of other sources, including the excavations at Hastinapur, seem to indicate that the battle was a purely local one fought between two Aryan groups.

Then we have the case of Mohammad who made no claims to performing any miracle other than bringing the Koran. However, posterity could not refrain from ascribing to him a miraculous birth and generally immersing him in the supernatural: Mohammad cast no shadow, his perspiration created the rose, he ascended to heaven on the winged horse Buraq, etc.

In the traditional Buddhist account of the life of Buddha, the Hindu God Brahma is seen descending from the heavens to plead with him to spread the new doctrine lest the world should perish. The fabrication and its purpose are transparent enough not to merit any further comment.

As for Jesus Christ, not only do we not have the foggiest notion as to what he really looked like, but tradition has also erred regarding the precise year of his birth. In this regard, it would be more revealing to know how the Bible, as we know it today, was allegedly compiled at the First Council of Nicea.

But first for the background: The young non-Christian Roman General Constantine, an aspirant to the throne, was pitted against the numerically superior force of a rival claimant, Maxentius. The night before the battle Constantine has a dream or vision in which he is commanded to conquer in the name of Christ. The following day Constantine has his 'pagan' soldiers carry the XP , the Greek symbol of Christ which is also a symbol of the pagan sun God Chronos and emerges victorious. Having become the emperor of Rome, he issues the decree of tolerance whereby Christians are permitted to pursue their faith free of the persecution they were subjected to earlier.

The Christians of the time are sharply divided on the true tenets of Christianity and in fact, on the very nature of its founder: was he a man or the only incarnate son of God, or both? Constantine wants the Church to be a politically integrating force, the cement of the empire, but first the Christians must settle their religious differences and arrive at a firm consensus. After all, if the Church is to provide effective support to the Roman Empire, it cannot afford dissension within its own ranks. It must speak with one clear voice. And so the First Council of Nicea is summoned in A.D. 325 with 300 religious leaders participating, in order to separate the grain of Biblical literature from its chaff.

Sybil Leek in her book 'Reincarnation: The Second Chance' describes what ensued. ''When agreement will not easily come about, it is decided to submit the matter to none other than Providence. All the books referred to the council for determination having been, in the words of the council historian Pupus, 'promiscuously put under the communion table of the church', the Lord is beseeched to place the inspired writings on the table, leaving the rest beneath, and 'it happened accordingly'!''Other sources tell us that five dissidents were banished, and anyone who did not deliver up his books to be burned was threatened with death.

Granting the validity of Sybil Leek's account, one is left wondering as to how accurately Jesus's life and teachings were transmitted to posterity.

Also in this context, the observations of the renowned scholar and Orientologist Proferssor F. Max Muller on what he terms the 'Dialogic Process' not only affords food for thought, but are, to my mind, incontestable: 'This...process as applied to the facts of history,' he explains, 'comprehends all the changes which are inevitably produced by the mere communication and interchange of ideas, by the give and take of dialogue, by the turning of thoughts from one side to the other...There is hardly a single fact in history which can escape being modified by this process before it reaches the writer of history. It must be distinguished from the Mythological Process, which forms indeed a part of it, but acts under much more special rules. We can watch the Dialogic Process in Modern History also, though we have here reporters, and newspapers, the autobiographies and reminiscences of great statesmen which would seem to render this Dialogic infection impossible or harmless. We can only guess what it must have been in times when neither shorthand nor printing existed, when writing and reading were the privilege of a small class...It is extra-ordinary that so many historians should have completely neglected this Dialogic Process through which everything must pass before it reaches even the first recorder, for-getting that it could never have been absent. How many difficulties would have been solved, how many contradic-tions explained, nay how many miracles would become perfectly natural and intelligible, if historians would only learn this one lesson, that we do not and cannot know of any historical event that has not previously passed through this Dialogic Process."

Swami Vivekananda's Guru Sri Ramakrishna ex-pressed the same idea in a different way: 'The Vedas, Tantras, and the Puranas, and all the s∶ ed scriptures of the world, have become as if defiled (as iood thrown out of the mouth becomes polluted) because they have been constantly repeated by and have come out of human mouths. But the Brahman or the Absolute has never been defiled, for no one as yet has been able to express Him by human speech.' Asked why religions degenerate, he answered: 'The rain-water is pure, but becomes soiled according to the medium it passes through. If the roof and the pipe is dirty, the discharge is dirty.'

A study at the world religions shows, that despite a common belief in a level of being that is higher than our ordinary or normal human state, there are numerous disparities which, at their face value, seem irreconcilable. Orthodox Christianity, for instance, refuses to have anything to do with the doctrines of rebirth and Karma set out later in this book, which are central to both Hinduism and Buddhism.

Here it is important, I think, to keep a few things in mind. The major world religions were founded many, many years ago, and we have already seen examples of the kind of distortion and modification that takes place in human hands. Now for some other considerations. In some of the Andaman and Nicobar islands off the coast of India there are still people who live in the Old Stone Age. Doubtless, they will have seen aeroplanes flying high over them. If we were able to communicate with them, we can be quite certain that their description of an aeroplane would differ radically from ours. They would be describing the same object, yet our description of it would probably be as incomprehensible to them as theirs would be ridiculous to us.

To communicate effectively, therefore, we have necessarily to take into account factors such as the sentiments, ethos, traditions, culture, mythology and level of civilization of the people we are communicating with. Since these are not constants but variables, what could be more natural than for the same truth to find a variety of expressions, so much so that, allowing for the astonishing diversity of the human race, they should sometimes even seem contradictory to one another?

This also brings us to the key distinction between esoteric and exoteric religion, the former's emphasis on knowledge being in sharp contrast to the latter's insistence on faith. Thus we find Jesus making a differentiation between the apostles and the multitude: 'Unto you it is given to know the mystery of the Kingdom of God; but unto them that are without all these things are done in parable: that seeing they may see, and not perceive; and hearing they may hear, and not understand.' And again, after the parable of the mustard seed we are told, 'Jesus preached his message to the people, using many other parables like these; he told them as much as they could understand. He would not speak to them without using parables; but when he was alone with his disciples he would explain everything to them.'

Esoteric religion, in contrast to its exoteric counterpart, claims to be the custodian of secret doctrines that are not recorded in the orthodox canons, but which, like a sensible father would not dream of handing over his automobile to his five-year-old child, are to be transmitted only to recognised initiates.

And so it is that the same apparent fact can have different connotations, depending on whether its interpretation is esoteric or exoteric. To cite an instance, the 'Bardo Thodol' or 'The Tibetan Book Of The Dead' was widely used in pre-communist Tibet as a breviary, and read and recited on the occasion of death. But for the initiate into the esoteric doctrine, it had a symbolic and far deeper significance: he had to die to the old ego of his past before he could be spiritually reborn. Similarly, the deities one encountered after death were nothing but deities to the uninitiated; but esoterically, they were projections of the human psyche. Implicity, therefore, Buddhists would see the Buddhist deities, Hindus the Hindu gods and goddesses, Christians the Christian angels or saviour, and Mohammedans the Muslim paradise, while the atheists' after-death visions would be as empty of heavens and divinities as his beliefs were when he was alive. In that sense, like the phenomenal world itself, the visions were both real and unreal—a concept that exoteric religion and pseudo-scientific thought, with its 'either-or' postures, might find difficult to grasp.

In passing it may be relevant to draw the reader's attention to books on after-death phenomena like 'Life After Life' by Dr. Raymond A. Moody, who studied more than a hundred subjects who had experienced clinical death and had been subsequently revived, and whose findings would appear to bear out the ancient Tibetan text's psychological analysis.

Interestingly, esoteric Christianity, as represented in the primitive Christian Gnostic Church and such 20th century developments as theosophy, shares with Hinduism and Buddhism a belief in Karma and rebirth, and Origen, (a learned and renowned pupil of St. Clement of Alexandria), who held the doctrines to be Christian, was excommunicated by the exoteric Church 299 years after his death. And yet inadvertent allusions to rebirth seem to remain in the Bible: 'When Jesus came into the coasts of Caesarea Philipi, he asked his disciples saying, "Whom do men say that I the Son of man am?" And they said, "Some say thou art John the Baptist; some Elias; and others Jeremiah or one of the prophets".'

The exoteric expressions of religion need to be viewed against the background of the intellectual outlook of the time and place and the circumstances in which they were formulated. To take a few cases in point, the rise of Buddhism coincided with the increasing disenchantment of the people with the caste rigidities and excessive ceremonialism of the dominant Brahmanism of those days; the Bhakti movements of Kabir and Guru Nanak owed something to the contact between Hinduism and Islam; and among the significant facets of Jesus's time were the prevailing situation of rebellion among the Jews, their appallingly poor living conditions in occupied Palestine, and their expectation of a coming saviour that this state of affairs generated.

Another point to bear in mind would be the crucial and unique role of symbolism in religious expression. Many of religion's deeper truths reached a state which we may term supersensuous and for which, therefore, the ordinary work-a-day language of the world was found to be inadequate. Because man has imagination, he can explain through metaphors, symbols, myths and legends what would otherwise be incomprehensible. And because religion by its very nature cannot do otherwise but describe one order of experience in terms of another, the symbolic aspect of religion may be described as the chief characteristic of religious expression. This factor cannot be overstressed if we are to work towards forging a much-needed unity of world religions.

A quotation from Herman Hesse, the 1946 Nobel Prize Winner for Literature, would seem singularly apt here: "The wisdom of all peoples is one and the same; there are not two or more wisdoms, there is only one. My only objection to religions and churches is their tendency to intolerance: neither Christian nor Mohammedan is likely to admit that his faith, though holy, is neither privileged nor patented, but a brother to all the other faiths in which the truth tries to manifest itself.'

It is unfortunate that myths are often passed off as religious history, and symbols are taken as the 'real thing' rather than what they represent. This not only betrays a woeful misunderstanding of human psychology, but since myths and symbols inevitably differ from culture to culture, they furnish false grounds for feelings of exclusiveness. Miraculous births, supernatural happenings, and the concept of the saviour are by no means the monopoly of any particular religion, but are, in fact, common to the myths of all religions and often of their various sects as well. While myths have been recognised as a basic constituent of human culture, the true religious spirit does not require of us that we abandon our common sense and treat myths as historical facts.

★★★

The religion of authority, as embodied in institutions, and the religion of the spirit, as personified in individuals who have sought or had a direct encounter with Truth, have seldom got along famously. Institutions, inherently, are outward oriented. In contradistinction to the individuals whose names or teachings they seek to perpetuate, and who were driven by the inner compulsions of their own experiences, they represent the social facet of human life rather than reflect the primacy of the inner factors. As the badge-and-banner-bearers of their particular sects, they lose in spiritual substance what they gain in organisational strength.

It is the mystics who best harvest the spiritual fruits of religion. Their number is legion, and there is no religion in which they have not appeared from time to time to enrich its meaning. Interestingly, whatever their religion, they often speak with a strikingly similar voice. Their case throws up the need for people to seek for themselves a direct perception of the truth, rather than fall back lamely on a passive acceptance of the premises of one's own culture. As the Buddha put it, "Be a lamp unto yourself, seek refuge within yourself and not outside."

**Gautam Sen**

# Prologue

THE TIME IS the nineteenth century. The place is India. A tremendous storm is gradually gathering force over the nation's cultural horizon. Very soon it will sweep through this stuffy land and inflame its flagging spirit.

Yes, the British are here. They are here as the harbingers of a new age, the modern age. They are here with a new technology, with new knowledge, new values and new beliefs. Their gauge is reason. Their creed is humanitarianism.

But is not British policy in India racist and reactionary? Are not railway carriages and park-benches marked, 'For Europeans Only'? Is not the country being progressively ruralized? Is she not being turned into an agricultural colony of industrial England? Is not unemployment rampant and increasing?

But that is the grand irony of the British presence in India. They have ushered in the modern age, but their representatives here fight the very forces they supposedly champion.

Why?

Because they themselves are not exactly modern. Back home in England they were the black sheep, the forces of reaction, the feudal bloodsuckers, who tried to hold back the influx of modernism but went hopelessly under. Here, in India, they still have a free field. The booty is rich. If they rule with an iron hand and encourage vested interests, proclaim themselves as the Master race or the Imperial race with the God given right to rule and subdue and if they crush the 'natives' the moment they raise their dark, ugly heads—then surely they can keep their heads above water.

But how long will it work? There are problems already rising to the surface.

Since the last quarter of the eighteenth century Western scholars, numismatics, archaeologists and epigraphists have begun to slowly push open the long-barred doors of India's ancient and glorious past. They have begun to sow the seeds of pride in the Indian bosom. The servile nation has now begun to nurse an ego and look the British in the eye.

And indeed, there is much in the country's past to be justifiably proud of. For was it not here, in the Indus Valley civilization, as it was in Persia, Mesopotamia, and Egypt, that civilisation was first born and developed? When people in Europe lived crudely in caves and jungles, with their faces painted blue, did not there exist here commodious houses and sophisticated cities? Was not cotton used here centuries before it reached the West? Did not art flourish in this land like it never did before, or after, till the classical age in Greece? Were not the immortal Vedas composed here? And the Upanishads, of which Schopenhauer the pessimist said that its study was the solace of his life, and would be the solace of his death? And the original versions of Aesop's fables and the Arabian Nights; and even the stories of Cinderella and Jack and the Bean Stalks? Was not the 'Zero' discovered here, as was the decimal place value system, and the use of the minus sign? And in algebra, were not letters of the alphabet used here first to denote unknown quantities?... and what else? Does it really matter? India has an enviable heritage and now, with her confidence restored, who can hold her back? All these days she has been presuming her inferiority. Now the scales have been peeled from her eyes. She is conscious of greatness. She must go out and prove it.

May be the Christian missionaries will retard this evolving process. How they gain admirers among the people. Look at them—how they help the downtrodden: the outcastes, the women, the lepers, the orphans, the tribal folk. Look at how they lash out against casteism, polygamy, child-marriage, and the low position of women. Look at how they win converts—not only among the poor, but among the English-educated Indian elite as well.

Something must be done, and done fast. But it must be done thoughtfully and wisely. It must be done without hurrying.

The missionaries are, after all, also spreading education. Along with individual Englishmen, orientalists, educationlists and journalists, they are drumming in the modern outlook into India's medieval mentality. Equalitarianism and individualism are fast gaining foothold in this caste-ridden land.

And the Government—how long can it hold back the march of education? They can limit it and pervert it to serve their utilitarian ends—the production of 'native' clerks for their expanding establishment—but may not the essence of Western thought and dynamism seep through the Indian brain? And the modern technology the British are introducing for themselves: the railways, for instance—will it not, in the long run, help to better this backward land?

Yes, the British are useful and necessary here, in spite of themselves. But we must not remain content with that. We must work for our own advancement. Then, someday, we can work for our freedom.

But first things first. Reform Hinduism. Bring it back to its Vedic purity. Its excrescences were the undoing of our past splendour, its purge may well be the beginning of our future glory. Back to the Vedas. Down with suttee: the Hindu shastras do not approve of it. Down with widowhood. Down with superstition. Down with unreason. Down with casteism. These are, one and all, enemies of progress. These are abject deviations from the true Hindu path. These are the very ideas that betrayed us in the past.

Spread education. Enlighten the people. Create a scientific outlook.

Thus, also spread the awareness about Rammohan Roy and Dayanand Saraswati.

And, similarly Swami Vivekananda. 'Modern India', said Subhas Bose, 'is Vivekananda's creation'.

'What has caused India's downfall?' Vivekananda asks. What has caused her stagnation? Where is her zest for life, her search for truth, her quest for adventures of the mind and body? Why has the sun set over the Indian horizon? Why this eerie darkness?

Because the caste-system, once functional and fluid, a token to the spirit of toleration and mutual co-existence, has petrified and dealt a death-blow to the last vestige of social unity. (Initially caste was broadly divided into the Aryans and the non-Aryans, with subdivisions among the latter. It was an attempt at assimilating the conquered race at a time when the normal procedure was to exterminate the vanquished race altogether).

Because the privileged elite, insulated from the masses, has turned physically and morally bankrupt.

Because, in Vivekananda's own words, 'we are imbeciles...we speak of many things, parrot-like, but never do them...we are lazy'.

Because India has secluded herself.

'I am thoroughly convinced', Vivekananda avers, 'that no individual or nation can live by holding itself apart from the community of others, and wherever such an attempt has been made under false ideas of greatness, policy or holiness, the result has always been disastrous to the secluding one'. 'Give and take is the law'. 'Expansion is life, contraction is death'.

Look at Europe. Such vast oceans of thought. So disciplined. So dynamic. So productive. So powerful. And yet with a fatal chink in its armour: sordid materialism.

'The Western people', declares Vivekananda, 'talk a great deal of the new theories about the survival of the fittest, and they think that it is the strength of the muscles which is the fittest to survive. If that were true, any one of the aggressive old world nations would have lived in glory today, and we, the weak Hindu, never conquered even one other race or nation, ought to have died out, yet we live here three hundred millions strong: We, of all nations of the world, have never been a conquering race, and that blessing is on our head, and therefore we live'.

Well-meant and earnest, no doubt, but not quite accurate.

Hindu India attained political unity only under the big dynasties. It attained that unity through conquests.

Samudragupta of the Gupta dynasty has been hailed as

India's Napoleon. Though a magnanimous warrior, and known for his spirit of toleration, he 'exterminated the immediate neighbours of his empire, particularly Ganapati Naga, King of Padmavati (Narwar in Gwalior) and rajas ruling between the *Jamuna* and the *Narbada*. He reduced the Kings of the Jungle (Central India according to Fleet) to bondage. He laid tribute on the frontier peoples east and west, from Assam...to the Punjab'. ('Ancient India and Indian Civilization' by Paul Masson—Oursel, Helena De William Grabowska, Philippe Sterne).

The son of Samudragupta, Chandragupta-II, conquered the country of the Malavas (Malwa), Gujarat, and Saurashtra (Kathiawar).

Harsha, though a great humanitarian, was an equally great conqueror, and even conquered Nepal.

Findings subsequent to Vivekananda's time have disproved the Swami even further: By the eighth century A.D., the empire of Sri Vijaya included Malaya, Ceylon, Sumatra, part of Java, Borneo, Celebes, the Philippines and part of Formosa.

Vivekananda is, after all, human. He has his blind spots. But he can praise virtue among foreigners when he recognizes it:

'Why is it that forty million Englishmen rule three hundred million people here? What is the psychological explanation? These forty million put their wills together and that means infinite power, and you three hundred million have a will each separate from the other. Therefore, to make a great future of India, the whole secret lies in organization, accumulation of power, coordination of wills'.

And again: 'The days of exclusive privileges and exclusive claims are gone...and it is one of the great blessings of the British rule in India. Even to the Mohammedan rule we owe that great blessing, the destruction of exclusive privilege'. 'My friends, it is no use fighting among the castes. What good will it do? It will divide us all the more, weaken us all the more, degrade us all the more.'

To the cyclonic young Swami, the road to national revival is clear: a new ethic of enquiry and self-criticism, a re-interpretation of Hinduism in the light of modern realities, a merging of what is best in Westernization with all that is noble in India's hallowed antiquity—for a nation can only grow in the light of its aptitudes and environment. You cannot grow against the grain:

'Each nation has its own part to play. In India, religious life forms the centre, the keynote of the whole music of national life'. 'Our vigour, our strength, nay, our national life is in our religion. You cannot get out of it, you have it now and for ever, and you have to stand by it, even if you have not the same faith that I have in our religion. You are bound by it, and if you give it up, you are smashed to pieces. That is the life of our race and that must be strengthened.'

Above all, you must identify yourself with the people, 'I consider the great national sin', he says, 'to be the neglect of the masses, and that is one of the chief causes of our downfall'. 'Go, all of you, wherever there is an outbreak of plague or famine, wherever the people are in distress, and mitigate their sufferings. At the most you may die in the attempt. What of that?'

And so the revolutionary departure from the age-old, exclusively inward-looking Hindu monastic tradition: the establishment of a mission of service, the Ramakrishna Math and Mission, an organization not dissimilar to that of the Christian fathers in India.

Was it not Vivekananda's Master Ramakrishna himself who said: 'The world is like the curled tail of a dog. Straighten it, and it will curl up again'? Implicity, it is futile entangling oneself with the temporal affairs of erring humanity. The thing to do is to isolate oneself, to practice austerities and penances, to contemplate God in meditation and seek personal salvation.

'Pooh!' thinks Vivekananda. ''You have not understood my Master. A fellow's duty lies in serving the god in others. Did I not cajole my Master once to show me the

way to nirvikalpa samadhi*?—and did he not twit me on
it, saying: 'Shame on you. I never thought you were
capable of seeking your own salvation—you, who has the
ability to do so much good to mankind'."

So much good to mankind: the spiritual regeneration of
India and the world. 'My ideal can be put into a few words,
and that is: to preach unto mankind their divinity, and how
to make it manifest in every movement of life'. The world
needs the genius of India as much as India needs skills
from foreign lands. If a millenium is ever to come to this
planet, it is to come through acts of sharing. Let the East
and West shake hands. Never mind Rudyard Kipling.

As Vivekananda sets forth on his grand mission, with
nothing but his intense faith, zeal and love for mankind to
sustain him, we may well imagine him humming to himself
the eternal song of the Sannyasin:

Have thou no home. What home can hold thee, friend?
The sky thy roof, the grass thy bed; and food
What chance may bring; well cooked or ill, judge not.
No food or drink can taint that noble self
Which knows itself. The rolling river free
Thou ever be, Sannyasin bold. Say 'Aum tat sat aum'.

*the highest stage of samadhi or superconscious state in which there is no
longer any perception of the subject or of the object.

# The Grand Symphony

THERE WAS A time when Narendra, then a caustic college Bohemian, was not exactly a great fan of God. For all he knew, even if there was a God, He must have long ago muttered a curse on his bumbling creation and gone to sleep.

> ...for the world, which seems
> To lie before us like a land of dreams, so various, so beautiful, so new,
> Hath really neither joy, nor love, nor light,
> Nor certitude, nor peace, nor help from pain;
> And we are here as on a darkling plain
> Swept with confused alarms of struggle and flight,
> Where ignorant armies clash by night.*

How could the All-Merciful permit this? And how much power did He really have? Could it be that He created man only to see him turn into a Frankensteinian monster? Well, then surely he wasn't worth a damn. Then surely religion was a mistake, a left-over from an ignorant past that was better left to rot.

Science was the new God. Religion just couldn't stand up to it. Idolatry and reason wouldn't see eye to eye. Evolution and Adam and Eve wouldn't mix. Science and a faith in a Supreme Being wouldn't go together: if God was the cause, and this universe the effect, then what was the cause of the cause? Didn't it, in its turn, become the effect? Or didn't this God have a cause? And if God did not have a cause, why need the universe have one?

And then, if all religions were revealed, which one was true? Hinduism or Christianity? Buddhism or Islam? Jainism or Judaism? Whose God was true? Who was doing the fibbing?

One by one Narendra studied each and every religion... and heaved a sigh of relief. Perhaps religion was not all stuff and nonsense, after all. Perhaps it did make some sense. At least they were all the same; that is, they said the same thing in different words:

*Matthew Arnold

'At the beginning of this century it was almost feared that religion was at an end. Under the tremendous sledge-hammer blows of scientific research, old superstitions were crumbling away like masses of porcelain'. 'For a time it seemed inevitable that the surging tide of agnosticism and materialism would sweep all before it.' 'Many thought the case hopeless and the cause of religion lost once and for ever. But the tide has turned and the rescue has come—what? The study of comparative religions. By the study of different religions we find that in essence they are one'.

But did that necessarily prove the existence of God? At best, that was interesting— it provided food for thought. But you could hardly call it conclusive. You could not root your life on a probability—plus. The ground was soft and slippery. You needed a firmer, a more solid base.

The only way out was to experience God yourself. Seeing is believing. 'Begin with disbelief; analyse, test, prove everything, and then take it'.

Yes, thought Narendra, I will unravel this mystery. I will yearn for Him and see if He is there to answer. Did not Jesus say, Ask, and it shall be given you; seek and ye shall find; knock, and it shall be opened unto you'?

And who was to come into Narendra's life now but Ramakrishna?

'Have you seen God?' Narendra asked him. He had put the same question to every religious teacher he had met so far, but they had evaded the question or answered in the negative.

'Yes', Ramakrishna promptly replied. 'I have seen Him as I am seeing you. In fact I have seen Him much more intensely'.

Ramakrishna sensed in Narendra the relentless stirrings of an earnest soul, and decided to open the doors of spirituality to the noble youngster. The story goes that he blessed Narendra with the beatific vision of the Eternal, so that Narendra's doubts at once dissolved, to give way to that profound peace that passes ordinary understanding.

'Incarnations', Vivekananda says, 'can transmit spirituality with a touch, even with a mere wish'. 'They are the Teachers of all teachers, the highest manifestations of God through man'. 'God understands human failings and becomes man to do good to humanity'.

He recalls the words of Krishna in the Gita: 'Whenever virtue subsides and wickedness prevails, I manifest Myself. To establish virtue, to destroy evil, to save the good I come from Yuga (age) to Yuga'.

To Narendra, Ramakrishna was 'Bhagawan' or God incarnate.

At the feet of his new guru he verified his belief in the grand harmony of all religions.

'In a potter's shop', his Master explained, 'there are vessels of different shapes and forms—pots, jars, dishes, plates—but all are made of one clay. So God is one, but is worshipped in different ages and countries under different names and aspects'.

But then, if all religions are really the same, what makes them seem so different?

The difference is in communication. Each according to his perception. When you talk to a person, you want to be understood. When you want to be understood, you talk relative to your audience's capacity to understand.

'We know', Vivekananda says, 'that there may be almost contradictory points of view of the same thing, but they will all indicate the same thing'. At this moment he happens to be speaking in a church, and the situation suggests to him an appropriate simile:

'Take four photographs of this church from different corners: how different they would look, and yet they would all represent this church.

'In the same way, we are looking at truth from different stand points, which vary according to our birth, education, surroundings, and so on. We are viewing truth, getting as much of it as these circumstances will permit, colouring the truth with our own heart, understanding it with our own intellect, and grasping it with our own mind. We can only know as much of truth as is related to us, as much of it as we are able to receive. This makes the difference between man and man, and sometimes occasions even contradictory ideas; yet we all belong to the same great universal truth'.

'I am the Self', says Krishna in the Gita, 'existent in the heart of all beings'. 'He who sees all beings in the Self, and the Self in all beings, hates none'.

Harmony on earth, therefore, has a cosmic significance.

'I am in every religion', Krishna adds, 'as the thread through a string of pearls. Wherever thou seest extraordinary holiness and extraordinary power raising and purifying humanity, know thou that I am there'.

Christ tells the common man, 'Pray to thy Father in Heaven'. Here God lives beyond the sky, separated from man. With the more advanced, Jesus resorts to a different idiom. 'The Kingdom of Heaven is within you', he says. Vivekananda opines that he meant 'God is immanent in nature. He is the God in us'. 'He compares God to the vine and living beings to its branches; and to St. John he says that the Father and the Son are one.'

St. Paul confirms this when he says, 'Your body is the temple of the Holy Ghost which is in you'. 'Know ye not that ye are the temple of God and that the spirit of God dwelleth in you?'

And therefore John's dictum, 'If a man say, I love God, and hateth his brother, he is a liar'.

Yes, Christ teaches us that we must love even our enemies. 'He that is without sin among you, let him first cast a stone'.

As for Islam, 'as soon as a man becomes a Mohammedan', Vivekananda tells his California audience, 'the whole of Islam receives him as a brother with open arms, without making any distinction, which no other religion does. If one of your American Indians becomes a Mohammedan, the Sultan of Turkey would have no objection to dine with him. If he has brains, no position is barred to him.'

Vivekananda does not recall, perhaps, the following passage from the Quaran, which proclaims his message of universality very eloquently:

There is not a people but a warner has gone among
   them
And every nation had a messenger,
And every nation had a guide,
And certainly We raised in every nation a messenger,
   saying Serve Allah and shun the devil,
To every nation We appointed acts of devotion which
   they observe.
For every one of you did We appoint a Law and a way!

Buddha, described as the first thorough-going agnostic,
championed his own brand of metaphysical solidarity.
Vivekananda says, "Some of the most beautiful epithets
addressed to Buddha that I remember are, 'Thou the
breaker of castes, destroyer of privileges, preacher of
equality to all beings''. Buddha saved a herd of sheep,
intended for a king's sacrifice, by throwing himself upon
the altar. He would not refuse a meal of boar's flesh*
offered by a despised Pariah, even though he knew that it
was contaminated. In fact, he subsequently developed
dysentery and died, but did not regret his actions until
then.

His peerless disciple Ashoka the Emperor in his twelfth
edict proclaims: 'He who does reverence to his own sect,
while disparaging the sects of others...inflicts the severest
injury on his own sect. Concord, therefore, is meritorious,
to wit, hearkening and hearkening willingly to the law of
piety as accepted by other people'.

Judaism holds that man is made in the image of God: 'I
have said, ye are gods and all of you are children of the
Most High'. The spirit of man is the candle of the Lord,
a candle which is to be lit with a divine flame.

'Why was man created one?' the Rabbis ask. They
themselves reply: "In order that no man should say to
another, 'My father was greater than thine'''.

Jews do not find it necessary for other people to accept
Judaism in order to lead a good life.

---

*Buddha's last meal is said to have consisted of sukara maddava. Some
  Buddhists interpret this as "boar's delight" — a kind of fungus which
  boars are very fond of.

And so on and so forth. One could go on endlessly, shifting from one religion to another, and yet bumping into substantial unities.

'That universal religion about which pilosophers and others have dreamed in every country, already exists. It is here', Vivekananda asserts. 'If the priests and other people that have taken upon themselves the task of preaching different religions simply cease preaching for a few moments, we shall see it is there. They are disturbing it all the time, because it is to their interest. You see that priests in every country are very conservative. Why is it so? There are very few priests who lead the people; most of them are led by the people and are their slaves and servants. If you say it is dry, they say it is so, if you say it is black, they say it is black'. 'What would be the fate of a priest who wants to give you new and advanced ideas and lead you forward? His children would probably starve, and he would be clad in rags. He is governed by the same worldly laws as you are'.

History is full of examples of wars being fought in the name of religion, of particular religions being propagated by the sword, of bloody riots and deep-seated enmity between the adherents of different religions and of their various sects. These unfortunate occurences have been the result not only of the politicization of religion, both by the state and the church, but also of the intolerance bred by man's psychological insecurity and his fanatical attachment to the symbols of his own religion. This fanaticism he mistakes for the religion itself, and which, because they are exclusive to his own religious culture, he looks upon as superior. The result is, as Swift noted, that 'we have just enough religion to make us hate, but not enough to make us love, one another'.

Says Vivekananda, 'you cannot make all conform to the same ideas: that is a fact, and I thank God that it is so. I am not against any sect. I am glad that sects exist, and I only wish they may go on multiplying more and more. Why? Simply because of this: If you and I and all who are present here were to think exactly the same thoughts, there would be no thoughts for us to think'. 'If we all thought alike, we would be like Egyptian mummies in a museum looking vacantly at one another's faces—no more than that!'

There should be no discord, but differences must exist. 'Variation is the sign of life, and it must be there'.

Now let us pause here and put this principle to the test. Is variety only the spice of life, or is it also its law? What do the physicists say?

There can be no motion without the interaction of two or more forces. Newton's third law of motion states that each and every action has an equal and opposite reaction.

So the very idea of motion embodies the presence of contrary forces. When you hold a stone in your hand, it presses down with a force which is equal to its weight on your hand. Obviously, your hand exerts an equal upward force on it to prevent it from falling.

The next question is: is motion essential to existence?

Everything in this universe is in motion—everything from the largest stars to the tiniest atoms in our bodies. What would happen if all movement came to an abrupt standstill? Why, 'Time' itself would disappear. 'Time' implies duration, which implies motion.

If time ceased, so would the universe, because the mass of a body depends on the time its particles take to travel. The faster they travel, the greater the mass of the body. Without motion, there would be no mass.

So motion is essential for existence. Contrary forces are essential for motion and hence, are essential for existence.

This contrariness or variety, Vivekananda contends, should be accepted as an inherent law of life, adding to its richness. But it should not degenerate into profanity and destruction:

'Sectarianism, bigotry, and its horrible descendant, fanaticism, have long possessed this beautiful earth. They have filled the earth with violence, drenched it often with human blood, destroyed civilization and sent whole nations to despair. Had it not been for these horrible demons, human society would be far more advanced than it is now'

Each religion supplements the other, animates it, endows it with the momentum which is indispensable to its survival.

'Our watchword, then, will be acceptance, and not exclusion', Vivekananda concludes. Toleration is not enough, for so-called toleration is often blasphemy, and I do not believe in it. I believe in acceptance. Why should I tolerate? Toleration means that I think you are wrong and I am just allowing you to live. Is it not a blasphemy to think that you and I are allowing others to live? I accept all religions that were in the past, and worship with them all; I worship God with every one of them, in whatever form they worship Him. I shall go to the mosque of the Mohammedans; I shall enter the Christian's church and kneel before the crucifix; I shall enter the Buddhist temple, where I shall take refuge in Buddha and in his Law. I shall go into the forest and sit down in meditation with the Hindu, who is trying to see the Light which enlightens the heart of every one.

'Salutation to all the prophets of the past, to all the great ones of the present, and to all that are to come in the future'.

'That's all very glib', you smile crookedly and say, "but I just don't believe it. Let's take an example: you Hindus practice idolatry, don't you? Well, I too am religious but my religion says, 'Beware of idolatry—it's a big, fat sin!' And yet you prattle on that all religions are the same. Tell me another!"

May be someday when I visit your home I'll walk up to your late mother's photograph on the shelf in your drawing room and spit pan*-juice on it. I can picture you then: alive and literally kicking—me! But I think I'm going to have the last laugh. I'm going to turn on you and say, 'But old chap, this is idolatry! This is not your mother, but a two-rupee image of hers—and yet you thought I was dishonouring her! Now, whatever's wrong with you?'

---

*The red juice of the betel-leaf, which is chewed together with betel-nut, catechu, lime, etc.

And then, if you're willing to listen, I'am going to spout Vivekananda on you: 'We are all born idolaters, and idolatry is good, because it is in the nature of man. Who can get beyond it? Only the perfect man, the God-man. The rest are all idolaters'.

You needn't growl. He has actually hit the nail on the head. If you need your mother's photograph just to remember her by, how much more you'll need an image of God, whom you haven't ever seen! And then, God is represented as Infinity, as you know. Our consciousness, however, is finite and, hence, necessarily limited. As far as we are concerned, Infinity is purely an intellectual abstraction. We inevitably think in terms of time and space. We visualize through forms. Yet Infinity, by definition, transcends these barriers of human conception. How then can we relate to It? Through symbols, of course. The point to note is that these symbols do not stand for themselves, but for a reality higher than themselves which our minds cannot grasp.

An idol is, therefore, as Vivekananda puts it, 'a peg to hang our spiritual ideas on'.

Throughout the history of the world, he says, 'we find that man is trying to grasp the abstract through thought-forms, or symbols. All the external manifestations of religion—bells, music, rituals, books, and images—come under that head.'

'Among the Jews idol-worship is condemned, but they had a temple in which was kept a chest which they called an ark, in which the Tables of the Law were preserved, and above the chest were two figures of angles with wings outstretched, between which the Divine Presence was supposed to manifest itself as a cloud. That temple has long since been destroyed, but the new temples are made exactly after the old fashion, and in the chest religious books are kept. The Roman Catholics and the Greek Christians have idol-worship in certain forms. The image of Jesus and that of his mother are worshipped. Among Protestants there is no idol-worship, yet they worship God in a personal form, which may be called idol-worship in another form. Among Parsees and Iranians fire-worship is carried on to a great extent. Among Mohammedans the prophets and great and noble persons are worshipped, and they turn their faces towards the Caaba when they pray. The Buddhists and the Jains, although they have no personal God, worship the founders of their religion in precisely the same way as others worship a Personal God'.

'Okay', you agree somewhat grudgingly, 'this time he wins, but I'm going to corner him now. Like take for instance Moses' watchword: 'A tooth for a tooth and an eye for an eye'. How the hell can he reconcile that with Jesus's 'If someone slaps you on the left cheek, offer him your right'?. or Buddha's saying: 'Even though robbers and murderers should sever your limbs and joints with a saw, if you therefore gave way to anger you would not be following my teaching. Thus rather, my disciples, ought you to behave: Your spirit should not be moved, no evil word should escape your lips; you should remain benevolent, with your heart full of love and void of secret malice; and you should enfold these men (the malefactors) with loving thoughts, with thoughts generous, deep, and limitless, purged of all anger and hate'. Mohammad was militant too, wasn't he? And perhaps Vivekananda has quite forgotten that in spite of all the wonderful things the Hindu scriptures say about peace, it was Krishna himself who urged Arjuna to fight''.

Vivekananda replies: 'The extreme positive and the extreme negative are always similar. When the vibrations of light are too slow, we do not see them, nor do we see them when they are too rapid. So with sound: when very low in pitch, we do not hear it; when very high, we do not hear it either. Of like nature is the difference between resistance and non-resistance. One man does not resist because he is weak, lazy, and cannot, not because he will not; the other man knows that he can strike an irresistable blow if he likes; yet he does not strike, but blesses his enemies. The one who from weakness resists not commits a sin, and as such cannot receive any benefit from the non-resistance, while the other would commit a sin by offering resistance'.

So what we must keep in mind is that an act by itself may not reveal as much as the thought or motive behind it. For example, let's suppose that both you and I run charity schools. You do it out of compassion for the poor, out of a heart-felt concern for their plight, whereas I do it because, I'm standing for the next state Assembly elections. My aim, actually, is to build up for myself a good public image. Our external actions are similar, and for all the world knows, I'm as virtuous as you are. But that, of course, is nonsense. I'm an inveterate selfseeker, while you're a humanitarian.

When we deal with Moses, Mohammad, Jesus or Buddha, how are we to reconcile differences in outlook as the one referred to earlier.?

Followers of the Baha'i Faith, a religion founded by Mirza Husayn Ali of Persia, believe that God reveals Himself through His messengers or 'manifestations'. They also believe that, while the essence of all religions is one, each has distinctive features corresponding to the needs of a particular time and place, and to the level of civilization in which a manifestation appears.

Vivekananda would seem to agree with them in this respect, for he asserts that 'to the Hindu, man is not travelling from error to truth, but from truth to truth, from lower truth to higher truth'. 'The child is father of the man. Would it be right for an old man to say that childhood is a sin or youth a sin?'

As for Krishna's counsel to Arjuna, he explains: 'Arjuna became a coward at the sight of the mighty array against him: his 'love' made him forget his duty towards his country and king. That is why Shri Krishna told him that he was a hypocrite: 'Thou talkest like a wise man, but thy actions betray thee to be a coward. Therefore, stand up and fight!' "

Now let us take the case of anger. Though from the perspective of the highest spiritual plane, anger is a wrong emotion, I can grasp this only intellectually. As far as my own life is concerned, I realise I cannot as yet do without anger, so I accept it and give it its due place. I've learnt it will simply not do to try to wish it away or pretend it's not there, because in so doing I'd only be destroying myself and those around me. Hidden anger can be much more killing than anger expressed, and anger expressed need not necessarily be destructive. I can work it off on a punching bag or by going for a walk or a run, and come back to the particular situation with a cooler head and a more balanced judgement.

Supposing I were to say, instead, 'Anger leads men to do evil', and to pretend to myself that I've transcended it. What would happen then?

Obviously, the food you eat but cannot digest doesn't disappear from your system. Rather, what you get is indigestion, and this, in turn, if untreated or treated inadequately, may lead to loss of appetite, insomnia, fatigue, bad temper or all these put together.

And so it is with anger or any other toxic emotion...fear, hatred, lust, greed, envy, jealousy, and what have you. Once it arises and you do not acknowledge its presence, you merely drive it into your subconscious, from where it works insidiously on your mind and your body and your relationships, destroying wherever it lays its hands. It's like syphillis. The initial eruptions may subside without treatment, but this is not a good sign—only a signal that the disease has progressed and will build up further in your system, whether you're aware of it or not.

Or its like a pressure cooker with its vent choked, asking for an explosion.

So when anger arises, what am I to do? The first essential, I think, is to recognise the fact, to acknowledge that it exists and give it my full attention. One has to go through anger before one can leave it behind. That may not be in accordance with someone's scripture, but that is where a person must begin. One must make one's peace with anger, so to speak.

In a similar vein, a passage in the Apocryphal Acts of John, a Gnostic book, reads: 'Had you known how to suffer, you would have been able not to suffer. Learn to suffer, and you shall be able not to suffer'.

In that sense, to repeat Vivekananda, man is travelling not from error to truth, but from lower truth to higher truth.

Returning to the question of inter-religious disharmony, Vivekananda asserts that, to a large extent, this blunder occurred because most of the religions have been indiscriminately divorced from their native soil. In order or demonstrate this point he takes up the case of Christianity:

'When the different religions came out from the motherland, they got mixed up with errors. The most profound and noble ideas of Christianity were never understood in Europe, because the idea and images used by the writers of the Bible were foreign to it'. 'I have seen hundreds of pictures of the Last Supper of Jesus Christ, and he is made to sit at a table. Now Christ never sat at a table, he squatted with others, and they had a bowl in which they dipped bread—not the kind of bread you eat today. It is hard for any nation to understand the unfamiliar customs of other people. How much more difficult was it for Europeans to understand the Jewish customs after centuries of changes and accretions from Greek, Roman, and other sources! Through all the myths and mythologies by which it is surrounded it is no wonder that the people get very little of the beautiful religion of Jesus. No wonder then that they have made of it a modern shop-keeping religion'.

So we come back to Vivekananda's postulate that 'there has been, and still is, one religion in the world, presenting different aspects in different pláces'. This standpoint has been partially corroborated by no less a scholar than Professor Arnold Toynbee, who 'expresses his personal belief that the four higher religions that were alive in the age in which he was living were four variations on a single theme and that, if all the four components of this heavenly music of the spheres could be audible on each simultaneously and with equal clarity to one pair of human ears, the happy hearer would find himself listening not to a discord, but to a harmony'.

# Treasure Island

## I

THE 'MODERN' MAN, I expect, steeped in what he genuinely considers 'the scientific outlook', impatiently flips through the previous chapter, grunts, tears out the pages, and deposits them in the nearest waste-paper basket. And he remarks to himself: 'A grand symphony, my foot! Rather, a racket of rusted, antiquated instruments! There is no god'.

'How do you know?' I ask.

'Well', he retorts, 'its simple. God was born in religion, and religion has no rational foundation. It all sprang up from the delusions of the primitive mentality. Primitive man was funked and insecure. He didn't have much of science and technology to control nature with. He felt overawed by the mighty cosmic forces that worked around him and was wholly at their mercy—they could screw up his scene any moment. And unintelligent and ignorant as he was, he turned them into gods and sought to appease them through prayers and sacrifices. Agreed, that with time, religion did become sophisticated and intellectualized, but its very foundations are cock-eyed, you see?'

This theory, still quite a popular one, is actually somewhat outdated. It is true that in the Rig-Veda Samhita, the most ancient record of the Aryan race, we do find ample evidence of nature-worship. It is not, however, triggered by feelings of alarm or fear, but rather by an urge to know and discover. As Vivekananda says of these times, 'the human mind seems to struggle to get a peep behind the scenes. The dawn, the evening, the hurricane, the stupendous and gigantic forces of nature and its beauties, which have exercised the human mind. The mind aspires to go beyond and understand something about them. In the struggle they endow these phenomena with personal attributes, giving them souls and bodies—sometimes beautiful, sometimes transcendent'.

Talking in the same vein, Rabindranath Tagore

describes the early Vedic Aryans as a 'people of vigorous and unsophisticated imagination awakened at the very dawn of civilization to a sense of the inexhaustible mystery that is implicit in life', in whom 'the sense of mystery only gave enchantment to life, without weighing it down with bafflement'.

Moreover, there are primitive cults elsewhere which are addressed to lizards and frogs, rabbits and ducks, and vegetables. If protection is what these people wanted, it is inconceivable that they worshipped such minor powers while neglecting the sun, the sky, the sea, the winds, and the like.

Tried as they may have, to go back to the origin of religion, the social scientists have not quite been able to do so. Their past assumption that present-day primitive peoples have no history, has been clearly disproved. And the various speculative theories about the origin of religion are now fast giving way to empirical descriptions and analyses, leaving religion's fundamentals untainted.

Vivekananda holds that 'the real germ of religion is the struggle to transcend the limitations of the senses'. 'Man continued inquiring more deeply into the different stages of the mind and discovered higher states than either the waking or the dreaming. This state of things we find in all the organised religions of the world, called either ecstasy or inspiration. In all organized religions, their founders, prophets and messengers are declared to have gone into states of mind that were neither waking nor sleeping, in which they came face to face with a new series of facts relating to what is called the spiritual kingdom. They realised things there much more intensely than we realise facts around us in our waking state. The Rishis (of ancient India) declared that they had realised—sensed, if that word can be used with regard to the supersensuous—certain facts, and proceeded to put them on record. We find the same truth declared amongst both the Jews and the Christians'.

'It may be asked—if the Buddhists do not believe in any God or soul, how can their religion be derived from this

supersensuous state of existence?' The answer to this is
that even the Buddhists find an eternal moral law, and that
moral law was not reasoned out in our sense of the word.
But Buddha discovered it, in a supersensuous state of
mind.

'Thus, a tremendous statement is made by all religions
that the human mind, at certain moments, transcends not
only the limitations of the senses, but also the power of
reasoning'.

Rationalism is all right, says Vivekananda. It has its
place in life. But it must not claim for itself an omnipotence
it does not possess. Science has every right to question
religion, to inspect it under its microscope, to chop out its
ugly excrescences, to discard what in the latter it finds
illogical and superstitious. But it may not encroach on
phenomena outside its grasp. Where reason ends, there
religion has just begun—the two are supplementary,
rather than incompatible.

'In the old Upanishads, we find sublime poetry. Plato
says inspiration comes to people through poetry, and it
seems as if these Rishis, (the poets of the Upanishads),
seers of truth, were raised above humanity to show these
truths through poetry. Music came out of their hearts. The
universal heart and infinite patience of the Buddha made
religion practical and brought it to everyone's door. In
Shankaracharya we saw tremendous intellectual power
throwing the scorching light of reason upon everything.
We want that bright sun of intellectuality joined with the
heart of Buddha, the wonderful infinite heart of love and
mercy. This union will give us the highest philosophy.
Science and religion will meet and shake hands. Poetry
and Philosophy will become friends. This will be the religion of the future, and if we can work it out, we may be
sure that it will be for all times and peoples'.

## II

You can fire a candle clean through a timber door. You
can cut through a thick block of wood with nothing more

than a whirling disc of thin tissue paper. Have you ever
watched a tornado?—even on a cinema screen? It
behaves like a regular solid, and what a solid! It picks up
rocks and hurls them hundreds of feet. It hews down
whole forests. It chops down the most majestic buildings
as if they were so much bamboo and hay!

How!

Motion can make even soft and flexible material hard
and stiff. Its form of energy is what gives a substance its
peculiar character. Einstein showed us how mass itself is a
form of energy, mass and energy being interchangeable
according to the formula $E=mc^2$.

The first chapter of the Bible says that matter came into
existence when 'the spirit of God moved'. This was
written so very long ago and yet is quite scientific in its
own way!

The ancient Hindu scriptures, too, hold that Spirit and
Matter are two extreme modes of the same existence.
Vivekananda words it this way:

'According to the philosophers of India, the whole universe is composed of two materials, one of which they call
Akasha. It is the omnipresent, all penetrating existence.
Everything that has form, everything that is the result of
combination, is evolved out of this Akasha. It is the
Akasha that becomes the air, that becomes the liquids,
that becomes the solids, it is the Akasha that becomes the
sun, the earth, the moon, the stars, the comets; it is the
Akasha that becomes the human body, the animal body,
the plants, every form that we see, everything that can be
sensed, everything that exists. It cannot be percieved; it is
so subtle that it is beyond all ordinary perception; it can
only be seen when it has become gross, has taken form. At
the beginning of creation there is only this Akasha.

'By what power is this Akasha manufactured into this
universe? By the power of Prana. Just as Akasha is the
infinite, omnipresent material of this universe, so is this
Prana the infinite, omnipresent manifesting power of this
universe...Out of this Prana is evolved everything that we
call energy, everything that we call force. It is the Prana

that is manifesting as motion; it is the Prana that is manifesting as gravitation, as magnetism. It is the Prana that is manifesting as the actions of the body, as the nerve currents, as thought force. From thought down to the lowest force, everything is but the manifestation of Prana. The sum total of all forces in the universe, mental or physical, when resolved back to their original state, is called Prana.. When there was neither aught nor naught, when darkness was covering darkness, what existed then? Then Akasha existed with motion. The physical motion of the Prana was stopped, but it existed all the same'.

One thing: It should be kept in mind that the Hindus do not believe in the religious 'Western' concept of creation insofar as they hold that something cannot come out of nothing. Creation is but a projection of a Something which already existed. That Something, of course, is God, the Fountain-Head from Whom both Akasha and Prana emanated.

Some men spy a loop-hole here. They ask, 'And pray, who or what created this God?'

The question, if you care to analyse it, betrays a contradiction in terms.

The word 'Absolute', which conveys the nature of God, necessarily implies that It exists by Itself. Vivekananda elucidates the point thus:

'This Absolute has become the Universe by coming through time, space and causation. Now we at once gather from this that in the Absolute there is neither time, space, nor causation. What we call causation begins after, if we may be permitted to say to, the degeneration of the Absolute into the phenomenal, and not before'. "The very asking of the question 'Why' presupposes that everything around us has been preceded by certain things and will be succeeded by certain other things". 'In asking what caused the Absolute, what an error we are making! To ask this question we have to suppose that the Absolute also is bound by something, that It is dependent on something, and in making this supposition, we drag the Absolute down to the level of the Universe'.

As Dionysius explains it, 'While God posses. attributes of the universe, being the universal Cau. in a stricter sense He does not possess them, since transcends them all'.

The Absolute, though transcendent, is also immanent in this world. It is, in fact, its essence. We are all one. Separation simply does not exist: it is a mirage. Whatever is, whoever is, is in God. God permeates the universe.

'Thou art the man', sing the Vedic sages, 'thou the woman, thou the young man walking in the strength of youth,...thou the old man tottering with his stick'.

Remember Wordsworth? His 'sense sublime of something far more deeply interfused, whose dwelling is the light of setting suns... and in the mind of man'?

Meister Eckhart: 'All blades of grass, wood and stone, are one'.

Plotinus: 'The One is all things and yet no one of them... for the very reason that none of them was in the one, are all derived from it'. 'Being perfect by reason of neither seeking nor possessing nor needing anything, the One overflows, as it were, and what overflows forms another hypostatis...How should the most perfect and primal good stay shut up in itself as if it were envious or impotent?... Necessarily then something comes from it'.

Jan wan Ruysbroeck says of the 'God-seeking man' that his spirit is 'undifferentiated and without distinction, and therefore it feels nothing but the unity'.

Jacob Bohme talks of the time when 'in this light my spirit saw through all things and I recognized God in grass and plants'.

For Spinoza, in God, quite literally, we live and move and have our being.

Emerson tells us: 'As one diffusive air, passing through perforations of a flute, is distinguished as the notes of a scale, so the nature of the great Spirit is single, though its forms be manifold, arising from the consequences of acts'. And again: 'We see the world piece by piece, as the sun, the moon, the animal, the tree; but the whole, of which these are shining parts, is the soul'.

servation on telepathy, Vivekananda
ou eyer noticed the phenomenon that is
nsference? A man here is thinking some-
nought is manifested in somebody else, in
e. With preparations—not by chance—a
nd a thought to another mind at a distance,
nind knows that a thought is coming, and he
receives it exactly as it is sent out. Distance makes no
difference. The thought goes and reaches the other man,
and he understands it. If your mind was an isolated something here, and my mind was an isolated something there,
and there were no connection between the two, how
would it be possible for my thought to reach you? This
shows that there is a continuity of mind, as the Yogis call
it. The mind is universal. Your mind, my mind, all these
little minds are fragments of that universal mind, little
waves in the ocean'.

We do not normally associate psi phenomena with the
so-called communist mentality, and in fact the 1956 Soviet
Encyclopedia dismissed telepathy as 'an antisocial idealistic fiction'. Yet, by 1963, the Kremlin's attitude had
undergone sufficient change for it to issue an edict giving
top priority to the biological sciences, among which was
included parapsychology. Through arrangement with the
Government of India, the Soviets invited Yogis to Russia
for laboratory studies, and the 'Popov group', which the
Soviets referred to as 'The Bio-Information Section of the
A. S. Popov All-Union Scientific and Technical Society of
Radio Technology and Electrical Communications',
began a crash programme on ESP in 1965.

Working independently in the United States, Mr. Cleve
Backster, Director of the Backster School of Lie Detec-
tion in New York, found that the killing of tiny shrimp set
off reactions in plants and other living things in the
surrounding area. Inspired by other 'discoveries' of a
similar nature, he concluded that there was some kind of
inherent 'primary perception' in all living things.

An article in the Winter 1974 issue of 'Horizon' carried a
discussion on 'the wierdest elementary particle of all'—

the neutrino. 'it has no magnetic field and no charge and no mass. It interacts with something else under the rarest circumstances—specifically, when a neutrino produced by the breakdown of boron-8 neulei hits a chlorine atom, the collision may produce an atom of radioactive argon. Otherwise, neutrinos are imperceptible; they pass through the earth as if it weren't there. So the neutrino hardly exists for us; but then we do not exist for it—Here, then, is a 'thing' almost devoid of the characteristics of matter coming to us from a different universe and probably (since it has no mass and is unaffected by gravity) moving through a different time continuum. Could mental energy be analogous to such particles?' 'Something like neutrino movement might possibly explain why the mysterious power of ESP transactions happens undisturbed by great distance, seemingly impenetrable hills, or thick walls'.

Coming back to the main topic, Vivekananda recalls "the old Persian story of how a lover came and knocked at the door of the beloved and was asked, 'Who are you?' He answered, 'It is I', and there was no response. A second time he came and explained, 'I am here', but the door was not opened. The third time he came, and the voice asked from inside, 'Who is there" He replied, 'I am thyself, my beloved', and the door opened. So is the relation between God and ourselves. He is in everything, He is everything. Every man and woman is the palpable, blissful, living God".

God is 'Satchidananda': Existence—Knowledge—Bliss.

If He is Existence, it must necessarily follow that we are in Him and He is in us. We are the effect and He is the cause, and the cause necessarily manifests itself as the effect. It is the same water that fills rivers, lakes and ponds, that is found in vegetation and that hides underground, that comes back to us in a different form as rain. Vivekananda cites his own example:

'Glass is produced out of certain materials and certain forces used by the manufacturer. In the glass there are those forces plus the materials. The forces used have become the force of adhesion, and if that force goes, the glass will fall to pieces; the materials also are undoubtedly in the glass. Only their form is changed. The cause has become the effect'.

'Very well!' you say, 'but then what's God's hide-and-seek all about? Is He all that modest and shy, or is He simply playful?'

When you were a raw stripling and first decided that true happiness lay between a girl's thighs, remember? You got up at six every morning and puffed away one solid hour at dumb-bells and calisthenics. You came back from school in the evenings and went for a run. You, who till yesterday couldn't spell the word 'routine', now became its greatest devotee. Sex was your goddess, and you served her well. Later, in college, when the thirst for knowledge gripped you, you skipped movies to buy your books and stayed up nights to read your favourite authors. Your idol had changed, but again you served it well, for you were a true devotee. You sacrificed, but you never knew it; you bore pain, but you took it in your stride. Your mind and heart had turned to hounds in the pursuit of your happiness. And so to every peak there is an ascent. And sometimes the climb is rugged and difficult, but the loyal seeker has the heart of a lion, and who can stop him?

God, they say, is bliss absolute—the highest peace, the highest happiness. One way or the other, isn't that what each of us is after? We are pilgrims at the altar of Fulfil-ment. But It does not show us Its face, and if it does, it's only for a wink!:

> The Worldly Hope men set their Hearts upon
> Turns Ashes—or it prospers; and anon,
> Like Snow upon the Desert's dusty Face,
> Lighting a little hour or two—is gone.*

The unanimous verdict of those seers and sages, belong-ing to different periods and different places, who have

*Omar Khayyam

sought and found the unitive knowledge of Godhead, points to the possibility of heavenly felicity even in this life. But, like in every craft, there is a method to be followed. There is no crash-course for realizing God. (Have you heard the modern man's prayer?—'Dear God, give me patience... and I want it this minute!). You must apply the proper means to reach the proper ends. You must follow the directions, or get disqualified:

'If any man will come after Me, let him deny himself, and take up his cross daily, and follow Me'. 'Blessed are the pure in heart, for they shall see God'.

If you want to reach God through the intellect, forget it! Don't even try! Says Vivekananda: "Religion belongs to the supersensuous and not to the sense plane. It is beyond all reasoning and is not on the plane of intellect. It is a vision, an inspiration, a plunge into the unknown and unknowable, making the unknowable more than known, for it can never be 'known'".

That remarkable intellect, Shankara, says in much the same tone: 'Erudition, well-articulated speech, a wealth of words, and skill in expounding the scriptures—these things give pleasure to the learned, but they do not bring liberation. A buried treasure is not uncovered by merely uttering the words 'come forth'..You must dig and work hard to remove the stone and earth covering it. Then only can you make it your own. In the same way, the pure truth of the Atman,* buried under maya and the effects of maya, can be reached by meditation, contemplation, and other spiritual disciplines such as one who knows Brahman** may prescribe—but never by subtle arguments!'

Vivekananda refers us to the Vedas: 'The Vedas teach us that the soul is divine, only held in the bondage of matter; perfection will be reached when this bond will burst and the word they use for it is, therefore, Mukti— freedom, freedom from the bonds of imperfection, freedom from death and misery.

'And this bondage can only fall off through the mercy of

---

* the soul
**the universal or absolute soul

God, and this mercy comes on the pure. So purity is the condition of His mercy. How does that mercy act? He reveals Himself to the pure heart; the pure and the stainless see God, yea, even in this life'. 'Then all doubt ceases'.

"The Hindu does not want to live upon words and theories. If there are existences beyond the ordinary sensuous existence, he wants to come face to face with them. If there is a soul in him which is not matter, if there is an all-merciful universal Soul, he will go to Him direct. He must see Him, and that alone can destroy all doubts. So the best proof a Hindu sage gives about the soul, about God, is: 'I have seen the soul; I have seen God'. And that is the only condition of perfection".

But what precisely is this 'purity' which opens the gates of Paradise in this very life.

Truthfulness; sincerity; doing good to others without any gain to one's self; not injuring others by thought, word, or deed; not coveting others' goods; not thinking vain thoughts; not brooding over injuries received from another. 'In this list', says Vivekananda, 'the one idea that deserves special notice is Ahimsa, non-injury to others. This duty of non-injury is, so to speak, obligatory on us in relation to all beings. As with some, it does not simply mean the non-injuring of human beings and mercilessness towards the lower animals; nor, as with some others, does it mean protecting cats and dogs and feeding ants with sugar—with liberty to injure fellow human beings in every horrible way! It is remarkable that almost every good idea in this world can be carried to a disgusting extreme. A good practice carried to an extreme...becomes a positive evil. The stinking monks of certain religious sects, who do not bathe lest the vermin on their bodies should be killed, never think of the discomfort and disease they bring to their fellow human beings'.

'The test of Ahimsa is absence of jealousy'.

Tall order? Too much trouble? This month you're too busy, you'll begin next month? Cut out the excuses and get down to work. 'Come up, O Lions, and shake off the delusion that you are sheep; you are souls immortal, spirits free, blest and eternal'.

This is the challenge thrown up by Vivekananda. Who will pick up the gauntlet?

'For God's sake hold your tongue!' you say. 'Please, the matter is not quite finished yet. I for one, think there's a stark fallacy in Vivekananda's proposition: If God is the Ultimate Perfection, as Vivekananda claims He is, and we're all part and parcel of that Perfection, how about all the evil and oppression around us? Where do they fit in?'

They fit into the dust-bin, really. They don't belong to us at all. They are the dust that has gathered on our spotless souls. Wipe it off and see what you really are.

Vivekananda would view the story of Adam and Eve not as a point of historical fact, but as a mythological representation of man's relationship with God. Man has freedom: he can choose to order his whole being in correspondence with Him, or, if he so desires, he can bite the fruit of the forbidden tree. But the responsibility is his and only his, and as he sows, so shall he reap.

'It is a significant fact', Vivekananda says, 'that all religions, without exception, hold that man is a degeneration of what he was, whether they clothe this in mythological words, or in the clear language of philosophy, or in the beautiful expressions of poetry. This is the kernel of truth within the story of Adam's fall in the Jewish scripture. This is again and again repeated in the scriptures of the Hindus: the dream of a period which they call the Age of Truth, when no man died unless he wished to die. When he could keep his body as long as he liked, and his mind was pure and strong. There was no evil and no misery; and the present age is a corruption of that state of perfection'.

Patently, man's fall is the consequence of his ignorant use of free will. Man is not bound by the shackles of a morbid and merciless Dictator, but by the fetters of his own indulgence.

Vivekananda can anticipate your next question: 'Why should the free, perfect and pure being be thus under the thraldom of matter?...How can the perfect soul be deluded into the belief that it is imperfect?'

"We have been told that the Hindus shirk the question and say that no such question can be there. Some thinkers want to answer it by positing one or more quasi-perfect beings, and use big, scientific names to fill up the gap. But naming is not explaining. The question remains the same. How can the perfect become the quasi-perfect? How can the pure, the absolute, change even a microscopic particle of its nature? But the Hindu is sincere. He does not want to take shelter under sophistry. He is brave enough to face the question in a manly fashion; and his answer is: I do not know. I do not know how the perfect being, the soul, came to think of itself as imperfect, as joined to and conditioned by matter'. But the fact is a fact for all that".

If he harps on the word 'Hindu' a bit too often, forgive him, for his was the hurt pride of a spirited soul in a colonised country—but, indeed, you do not have to know how a car runs to know that it does run; you do not need to know why we have two hands and not four to know that we do have only two. Our convictions are rooted in experience and are, therefore, convictions. Science requires us to adopt an empirical attitude, and it is only after Vivekananda believed what he saw, that he believed.

Here, in fact, lies the theoretical difficulty of his system. As William James explains it, 'It accredits itself by appealing to states of illumination not vouchsafed to common man. The regular mystical way of attaining the vision of the One is by ascetic training, fundamentally the same in all religious systems. But this ineffable kind of Oneness is not strictly philosophical, for philosophy is essentially talkative and explicit'.

However, the ascetic discipline is not perhaps as formidable and impracticable as it sounds. Like the time you went girl, or book chasing, your fire will doubtless be fanned by every small victory you achieve. Aurobindo's early experiences are a case in point:

'If God exists, then there must be some way which would lead one to experience his existence, to see him face to face. I have determined to tread the path that leads to God, however difficult it might be. The Hindu Dharma declares that that path lies in one's own body, in one's own mind. It has also laid down the rules which ought to be observed. I have started observing all those rules. Within a month, I have been able to testify to the truth of what Hindu Dharma has laid down. I am seeing and experiencing all the signs that it has indicated'.

It is not imperative that you lock yourself up in a remote monastery or retire to the seclusion of a cave to practise Yoga, the science of emancipation. It can be done even amidst the bustle of life, adding spice to the routine of daily existence, bringing you a fresh poise, a new orientation to the world around you. Whatever it is that you do, you will be able to do so much better.

There are, of course, other mystical techniques peculiar to different disciplines. Jesus, for instance, 'spake a parable unto them to this end, that men ought always to pray, and not to faint'. This is the method of incessant inner prayer or 'prayer of the heart'. The prayer is endlessly repeated by the mind in the heart, leading to physical sensations of spiritual warmth and the gradual access to new insights. Once we open ourselves to these insights, they are said to change the very course of our lives.

There's an island somewhere with a lot of treasure to be picked up. Won't you board the ship that takes you there?

### III

Karl Marx called it the opiate of the people. Applied properly, Vivekananda would say, religion is no opium— it is, rather, the supreme tonic. He would borrow, perhaps, Emerson's eloquent metaphor of organic dependance and say, 'As a plant upon the earth, so a man rests upon the bosom of God; he is nurtured by unfailing fountains, and draws at his need inexhaustible power'.

This is the power that our Swami himself imbibed, the power which enabled him to declare:

'I have a message for the world, which I will deliver without fear and care for the future. To the reformers I will point out that I am a greater reformer than any one of them. They want to reform only little bits, I want root-and-branch reform'.

This is the poise that enabled him to continue with his lecture, undisturbed, when in a cattle town in the western United States a group of doubting cowboys, testing his equanimity, whizzed bullets around his head.

For what is fear to that blessed man who has seen deep beyond the surface of life into the common essence of all things?

"When man has seen himself as One with the Infinite Being of the universe, when all separateness has ceased, when all men, all women, all angels, all gods, all animals, all plants, the whole universe has been melted into that Oneness, then all fear disappears. When to fear? Can I hurt myself? Can I kill myself? Can I injure myself? Do you fear yourself? Then will all sorrow disappear. What can cause me sorrow? I am the One Existence of the universe. Then all jealousies will disappear; of whom to be jealous? Of myself? Then all bad feelings disappear. Against whom shall I have this bad feeling? Against myself? There is none in the universe but me...kill out this differentiation, kill out this superstition that there are many. He who, in this world of many, sees that One; he who, in this mass of insentiency, sees that One Sentient Being; he who in this world of shadow, catches that Reality, unto him belongs eternal peace, unto none else, unto none else".

Man, ill-proportioned man: all brains, but with a lost soul. He has lost his equilibrium and, like an egg balanced on its end, can easily be knocked over. Man, miserable man, who has forgotten how to be happy, whose obsession has become, therefore, to remain obsessed with frivolities. Like the pilot somewhere over the Pacific who said, 'I'm lost, but I'm making record time!'

'There is no duty we so much underrate', as Robert Louis Stevenson says, 'as the duty of being happy'.

Is there, then, a way out?

There is an island, it is said, with endless treasure. If you can make good weather of it and cross the mighty spiritual sea, if you can pick up some of that priceless stuff, you can roll in riches for eternity—for that island is the end of misery:

'Where is there any more misery for him who sees this Oneness in the universe, this Oneness of life, Oneness of everything?...This separation between man and man, man and woman, man and child, nation from nation, earth from moon, moon from sun, this separation between atom and atom is the cause really of all the misery, and the Vedanta says this separation does not exist, it is not real. It is merely apparent, on the surface. In the heart of things there is unity still. If you go inside you find that unity between man and man, women and children, races and races, high and low, rich and poor, the gods and men: all are One, and animals too, if you go deep enough, and he who has attained to that has no more delusion...Where is there any more delusion for him? What can delude him? He knows the reality of everything, the secret of every- thing. Where is there any more misery for him? What does he desire? He has traced the reality of everything unto the Lord, that Centre, that Unity of everything, and that is Eternal Bliss, Eternal Knowledge, Eternal Existence. Neither death nor disease nor sorrow nor misery nor dis- content is There'.

'The materialist is right! There is but One. Only he calls that One Matter and I call it God'.

Whatever they might say, take it from our Swami, ignorance is not bliss, knowledge is.

# Religion And Society

WHAT IS PROGRESS? Air-conditioners, refrigerators? Electronic gadgets, artificial fertilizers? T.V. sets, skyscrapers, aeroplanes? Man walking on the moon? More education, more food, more clothes? Biological evolution?

'Yes, indeed', you say. 'Progress is the amoeba becoming man. Progress is economic and technological advancement. All this is progress'.

Progress for what? Progress for its own sake? That's downright nonsense. Progress is not the end; it is the means to the end. The end, the eternal end is happiness, fulfilment. Do your criteria satisfy this goal?

Let's take biological evolution. We shall now stand aside and hear Mr Bertrand Russell speak:

'Since evolution became fashionable, the glorification of man has taken a new form. We are told that evolution has been guided by one great purpose: through the millions of years when there were only slime, or tribolites, throughout the ages of dinosaurs and giant ferns, of bees and wild flowers, God was preparing the great Climax. At last, in the fullness of time He produced Man, including such specimens as Nero and Caligula, Hitler and Mussolini, whose transcendent glory justified the long painful process. For my part, I find even eternal damnation less incredible, certainly less ridiculous, than this lame and impotent conclusion which we are asked to admire as the supreme effort of Omnipotence'.

Mr. Russell concludes that 'mankind...are a mistake'.

This sullen outburst stems, no doubt, from an understandable sense of frustration at mankind's self-created plight. But at the same time one cannot quite help feeling that, in this instance, Mr Russell's overwrought emotions have got the better of his acknowledged powers of reasoning. Surely Aldous Huxley makes a very valid point when he observes:

'This is a world in which nobody ever gets anything for nothing. The capacity to go higher is purchased at the expense of being able to fall lower. Only an angel of light can become the prince of darkness. On the lower levels of evolutionary development there is no voluntary ignorance or deliberate evil-doing; but, for that very reason, there is also no enlightenment. That is why, in spite of Buchenwald and Hiroshima, we have to give thanks for having achieved a human birth'.

Vivekananda's views on evolution seem ambiguous in one respect. On the one hand he says, 'we often hear that it is one of the features of evolution that it eliminates evil, and this evil being continually eliminated from the world, at the last only good will remain. That is very nice to hear, and it panders to the vanity of those who have enough of this world's good, who have not a hard struggle to face every day, and are not being crushed under the wheel of this so-called evolution. It is very good and comforting indeed to such fortunate ones...Very well, yet this argument is fallacious from beginning to end. It takes for granted, in the first place, that manifested good and evil are two absolute realities. In the second place, it makes a still worse assumption, that the amount of good is an increasing quantity, and the amount of evil is a decreasing quantity'; on the other hand, he predicts that 'in time to come Christs will be in numbers like bunches of grapes on a vine; then the play will be over and will pass out. As water in a kettle beginning to boil shows first one bubble, then another, then more and more until all is in ebbulition and passes out as steam. Buddha and Christ are the two biggest 'bubbles' the world has yet produced. Moses was a tiny bubble, greater and greater ones came. Sometime, however, all will be bubles and escape; but creation, ever new, will bring new water to go through the process all over again'.

In the light of the theory of rebirth it is logical to conceive of a time when each person will finally attain liberation. We are all seeking perfection, whether we are aware of it or not. We are all reaching out for something eternal, and that something has to be infinite, because only the infinite can be eternal. We progress empirically, through a process of partial errors and partial truths. Our experiences are, in the long run, never wasted,, and the wiser we are the quicker can we grasp the essential purport of our pursuit, and the quicker can we reach our destination. Over the spread of numerous years and numerous lives it is inevitable, however unintelligent we might be, that we should come nearer our desired end than when we started. The clever travel fast, fools travel slowly, but we all travel and ultimately arrive at Infinity. Slowly but surely, man realizes the God in him, and the animal becomes man, to fulfil itself in its own turn. Religion is the chemical that catalyzes the transformation, for religion is nothing if not the search for the Ultimate Truth, the Ultimate Reality.

'Today the evolution theory of the ancient Yogis will be better understood in the light of modern research', says Vivekananda. 'And yet the theory of the Yogis is a better explanation. The two causes of evolution advanced by the moderns, viz. sexual selection and survival of the fittest, are inadequate. Suppose human knowledge to have advanced so much as to eliminate competition, both from the function of acquiring physical sustenance and of acquiring a mate. Then, according to the moderns, human progress will stop, and the race will die. The result of this theory is to furnish every oppressor with an argument to calm the qualms of conscience. Men are not lacking who, posing as philosophers, want to kill out all wicked and incompetent persons (they are, or course, the only judges of competency) and thus preserve the human race! But the great ancient evolutionist, Patanjali, declares that the true secret of evolution is the manifestation of the perfection which is already in every being; that this perfection has been barred and the infinite tide behind is struggling to express itself. These struggles and competitions are but the results of our ignorance, because we do not know the proper way to unlock the gate and let the water in. ('The water for irrigation of fields is already in the canal, only shut in by gates. The farmer opens these gates, and the water flows in by itself, by the law of gravitation. So all progress and power are already in every man; perfection is man's nature, only it is barred in and prevented from taking its proper course. If anyone can take the bar off, in rushes nature. Then the man attains the powers which are his already'). This infinite tide must express itself; it is the cause of all manifestation. Competitions for life or sex-gratification are only momentary, unnecessary, extraneous effects, caused by ignorance. Even when all competition has ceased, this perfect nature behind will make us go forward until every one has become perfect.'

When that has been obtained, man is fulfilled; but that boundless freedom does not come merely for the asking. It has to be worked for through the virtuous life:

'By their fruits ye shall know them…Not every one that saith unto me, Lord, Lord, shall enter the kingdom of heaven; but he that doeth the will of my Father who is in heaven'.

Is this call of Jesus a call to forsake one's individuality? Pandit Jawaharlal Nehru decidedly thinks so:

'It has always seemed to me a much more magnificent and impressive thing that a human being should rise to great heights, mentally and spiritually, and should then seek to raise others up, rather than that he should be the mouthpiece of a divine or superior power. Some of the founders of religions were astonishing individuals, but all their glory vanishes in my eyes when I cease to think of them as human beings. What impresses me and gives me hope is the growth of the mind and spirit of man, and not his being used as an agent to convey a message'.

Sorry Panditji, but here you have revealed your lack of metaphysical footing. You conceive of God and human beings as distinct entities; you cling to your ego, so to speak, and wrap it around yourself; you reject the possibility of religious self-realization and, by so doing, reject religion. For religion begins with the notion of a non-physical entity in man, which it represents as the real 'Self', a part of the infinite and therefore infinite in its own right, held in the prisonhouse of matter—the body. This non-physical entity knows no barriers of human individuality, for its individuality is undifferentiated and truly limitless. The God-man is not a tout of a Higher Being. He is a man who has dug beneath the surface of his apparent self and discovered his divine nature. And so it is that Vivekananda says:

'Each soul is a star, and all stars are set in that infinite azure, that eternal sky, the Lord. There is the root, the reality, the real individuality of each and all. Religion began with the search after some of these stars that had passed beyond our horizon and ended in finding them all in God, and ourselves in the same place'.

And again:

'The aim and end of all religions, is but one—reunion with God, or, what amounts to the same, with the divinity which is every man's true nature.'

Does this not echo the words of Christ?—'I am in my Father, ye in me, and I in you'.

So we see that biological evolution is progress, if only because it can open the door to spiritual evolution. Whether or not the mystical claim of unitive knowledge with the Godhead is authentic or otherwise, whether it is self-delusion or a 'supramental' fact, we ourselves can personally test and judge. The process is by no means unknown to the sciences—in geometry, for instance, where you often start with a hypothesis and then lead up to the proof. Meanwhile, if one takes a stand against mysticism, it does seem a trifle odd that mystics all over and at all times have preached similar concepts and virtues.

Vivekananda meets the sceptics with the rejoinder that we can at once recognise superconsciousness by the fruits it yields. 'An idiot, when he goes to sleep, comes out of sleep an idiot or even worse. But another man goes into the state of meditation, and when he comes out he is a philosopher, a sage, a great man. That shows the difference between these two states'.

Significantly Buddha, who admits of no God, yet admits of a supersensuous reality.

We now arrive at our next point; technological advancement. Too much of civilization has been a process of creating artificial wants and then chasing them. The more one relies on extraneous factors, the more dependant one becomes on them. A person habituated to cigarettes may find it terribly upsetting if, for some reason or other, none is available when he feels like smoking. Add to that the prospects, thanks to modern technology, of being able to destroy two-thirds of the world at a go, by the mere pressing of a little button. The pitfalls are far too numerous. Or take again, for instance, the manufacture of artificial fertilizers. No doubt they produce bumper harvests; but meanwhile, as Aldous Huxley says, 'they kill the indispensable earthworm and, in the opinion of a growing number of authorities, tend in the long run to reduce the fertility of the soil and to impair the nutritive qualities of the plants that grow on it'. 'New chemicals for the control of insects, viruses, and fungi seem to work almost miraculously, but only until such time as mutation and natural selection produce new and resistant strains of the old enemies'.

Similarly, the manufacture of a vast variety of drugs and medicines and their easy availability is also one of the reasons why many people pop pills at the slightest hint of indisposition, thus lowering their constitutional tolerance.

Of course, the creation of technology was by itself a great thing. As a reflection of man's ingenuity, and as a means through which man's creativity may flower, technological progress is always a welcome phenomenon. It can help secure basic physical and mental needs—food, water, housing, education, leisure, etc.—and open up avenues, and the will, for intellectual and spiritual development. How well these opportunities are exploited is another matter, but what is significant is that technological advancement does create the objective conditions for such growth. By itself, however, it affords an extremely myopic view of progress, and must therefore not be blown up out of proportion. Having reached dizzy heights in technology, man has made himself its slave. That is what is regrettable.

Religion is the foundation on which we must built. If this foundation is lacking, then the structure of our lives, however seemingly beautiful or impressive, is deemed to collapse under strain.

Who can ignore the importance of economic and political measures to secure human betterment? 'But', warns Vivekananda, 'one must admit that law, government, politics are phases not final in any way'. 'Objective society will always be a mixture of good and evil'. 'All the social upheavalists, at least the leaders of them, are starting to find that all their communistic or equalising theories must have a spiritual basis, and that spiritual basis is in the Vedanta only. I have been told by several leaders (in America and England) who used to attend my lectures, that they required the Vedanta as the basis of the new order or things'. (More recently Andre Malraux commented that 'the problem of this century is the religious problem, and the discovery of Hindu thought will have a great deal to do with the solving of that particular problem'). 'The basis of all systems, social or political, rests upon the goodness of men'. 'Religion goes to the root of the matter. If it is right, all is right'.

That presupposes, of course, that it can be wrong. Freud and Freudians, with their obsession with mental patients, allege that religion is inherently erratic. It constitutes a false security, and the sooner one gets rid of it, the better.

It is too true that there are neurotics galore roaming this world, and it is also too true that—what with increasing mechanization and its step-brothers, impersonality and loneliness (Albert Schweitzer noted that modern man is so much a part of a crowd that he is dying of a personal loneliness)—their numbers are snowballing day by day. But the crutch they choose to lean upon only happens to be, in this case, religion, or what passes in the name of religion.

Religion is an inward growth towards spiritual independence. If it is used as a crutch, it is not a religion at all.

Religion is man's greatest ally, and the extent to which it

can help us is directly proportional to the extent to which we can cultivate it. 'One ounce of practice', says Vivekananda, 'is worth a thousand pounds of theory'. Religion is realization. Without it, it is nothing. Political and social systems are beneficial or harmful according to the degree to which they support or contradict its cause.

A reporter to Vivekananda: 'Do not Hindus stand in need of social reform?'

Vivekananda: We do stand in need of social reform—kings have gone, the power is the people's. We have, therefore, to wait till the people are educated, till they understand their needs and are ready and able to solve their problems. The tyranny of the minority is the worst tyranny in the world'. 'We had better go to the root of the evil and make a legislative body, that is to say, educate our people so that they may be able to solve their own problems'.

Political systems gain his attention in so far as they have the power to stabilize society, for though a spiritual way of life is not really impossible under any conditions whatsoever, 'too much wealth or too much poverty is a great impediment to the higher development of the soul'. 'Religion is not for empty bellies', yet 'every human being has the right...to seek religion;.

Probably the most salient feature of Vivekananda's philosophy, as of Marx's is his activist theory of knowledge: philosophy is not talk or retrospection, it is action.

Vivekananda: 'The vast majority of men are athiests. I am glad that, in modern times, another class of athiests has come into existence in the Western world—I mean the materialists. They are sincere athiests. They are better than the religious athiests, who are insincere, who fight and talk about religion, and yet do not want, never try to realise it'. 'If I am in a dark room, no amount of protestation will make it any lighter—I must light a match'. 'Religion is not in doctrines, in dogmas, nor in intellectual argumentation; it is being and becoming, it is realisation'.

And now Marx: 'All philosophies have sought to explain the world; the point, however, is to change it'.

Marx's scientific materialism' has, however, turned out to be somewhat unscientific and untenable. He held it as axiomatic 'that the material world is the fundamental reality, and though it is accessible to thought, it is not constituted by it*— an inference, as we have seen previously, and as we shall see again later, that is utterly deluding. The notable scientist James Jeans comments that 'the universe begins to look like a great thought rather than a great machine', and no less a person than Albert Einstein observes that 'in this materialistic age of ours, the serious scientific workers are the only profoundly religous people'. It is interesting to note that Vivekananda regarded modern science as a manifestation of the real religious spirit, for it sought to understand truth by sincere effort.

Again, when Einstein remarks that 'the fate of the human race is more than ever dependant on its moral strength today. The way to a joyful and happy state is through renunciation and self-limitation everywhere', he might well be mistaken for our Swami himself. Says Vivekananda, "Ethics always says, 'Not I, but thou'. Its motto is, 'Not self, but non-self'. The vain ideas of individualism...have to be given up...You have to put yourself last, and others before you. The senses say, 'Myself first'. Ethics says, I must hold myself last. Thus, all codes of ethics are based upon this renunciation".

Marx posits that the ethical values of a community always mirror the interests of the dominant class and are therefore nothing but expressions of 'class morality'. Undoubtedly Vivekananda would concur with R. N. Carew Hunt when the latter counters the Marxian generalisation with the observation that 'this is to reject the existence of any objective standard. Every great work of literature reflects the social condition of its age; but it also contains aesthetic values which are universal. Equally, there are absolute and immutable ethical principles which have commended assent all down the centuries. For underlying the flux of history there is...a certain continuum to which all ethical judgements can be related, and

*R. N. Carew Hunt

which lead men to agree that Socrates was a good man and Nero a bad man, and that truth and charity are better than falsehood and malice. At all times men have agreed that it is better to assist their fellow creatures than to injure them...'. 'The ideology of marxism itself derives from men who, like Marx and Engels, were bourgeois and not proletarians'.

Since ethics is the fulcrum of Vivekananda's philosophy, it is pertinent to inquire whether there is such a thing as communist ethics. Lenin takes up the question: 'Is there such a thing as Communist ethics? Is there such a thing as Communist morality? Of course there is. Often it is made to appear that we have no ethics of our own, and very often the bourgeoisie accuse us Communists of repudiating all ethics. This is a method of shuffling concepts, of throwing dust in the eyes of the workers and peasants.

'In what sense do we repudiate ethics and morality?

'In the sense that they were preached by the bourgeoisie who declared that ethics were God's commandments. We, of course, say that we do not believe in God, and that we know perfectly well that the clergy, the landlords and the bourgeoisie spoke in the name of God in order to pursue their own exploiters' interests. Or instead of deducing these ethics from the commandments of God, they deduced them from idealistic or semi-idealistic phrases, which were always very similar to God's commandments.

'We repudiate all such morality that is taken outside of class concepts. We say that this is deception, a fraud, which clogs the brains of the workers and peasants in the interest of the landlords and capitalists.

'We say that our morality is entirely subordinated to the interest of the class struggle of the proletariat. Our morality is derived from the interests of the class struggle of the proletariat.

'...We say: Morality is that which serves to destroy the old exploiting society and to unite all the toilers around the proletariat, which is creating a new Communist society'.

Now let us consider Vivekananda's case. He shuns priestcraft, with which the Marxists invariably and erratically identify religion.

'Priestcraft and tyranny go hand in hand', Vivekananda says, and propagates a procedure of self-realisation that has nothing whatsoever to do with any institutional order but is, rather, entirely a matter of individual pursuit.

Lenin's statement saying, 'We, of course, say that we do not believe in God' would, from Vivekananda's standpoint, hardly disprove His existence. The proof of the pudding is in the eating. 'Seek, and ye shall find'.

As for the age-old question of the means and the ends, Vivekananda says: 'One of the greatest lessons I have learnt in my life is to pay as much attention to the means of work as to its end…Our greatest defect in life is that we are so much drawn to the ideal, the goal is so much more enchanting, so much more alluring, so much bigger in our mental horizon, that we lose sight of the details altogether.

'But whenever failure comes, if we analyse it critically, in ninetynine per cent of cases we shall find that it was because we did not pay attention to the means…With the means all right, the end must come. We forget that it is the cause that produces the effect; the effect cannot come by itself; and unless the causes are exact, proper, and powerful, the effect will not be produced. Once the ideal is chosen and the means determined, we may almost let go the ideal, becuase we are sure it will be there, when the means are perfected. When the cause is there, there is no more difficulty about the effect, the effect is bound to come'.

Vivekananda would straightaway reject the basis of Hegel's dialectics, on which Marx props his own. According to Hegel, contradiction (the thesis-antithesis phenomenon) is the motive force behind all development (synthesis). 'The thesis affirms a proposition. The antithesis denies, or in Hegelian terminology 'negates' it. The synthesis embraces what is true in both the thesis and the antithesis, and thus brings us one step nearer to reality.

But as soon as the synthesis is subjected to a closer inspection, it, too, is found defective; and thus the whole process starts over again with a further thesis, negated in turn by its antithesis and reconciled in a new synthesis. In this triangular manner does thought proceed until at last we reach the Absolute, which we can go on contemplating forever without discerning in it any contradiction'.* 'In Hegel's system the Absolute is the totality not only of thought but of all experience, that is, it includes time and all that has accured in time'. Thus nature, and 'the passage of events which we call history ... will exhibit that same dialectical inter-connection which has shown to be a property of the forms of thought'.

But, Vivekananda argues, how on earth can the finite become infinite? 'The analysis of the position of these philosophers is this that the Infinite is trying to express itself in this universe and that there will come a time when the Infinite will succeed in doing so. It is all very well, but the philosophers naturally ask for a logical fundamental basis for the statement that the finite can fully express the Infinite'.

It might be good to re-define the doctrine of Maya here in a nutshell: 'In the objective society there will always be a mixture of good and evil—objective life will always be followed by its shadow, death. In objective life every bullet has its billet—evil goes with every good as its shadow. The mixture of good and evil, of life and death, knowledge and ignorance is what is called Maya or the universal phenomenon'.

Hegel's 'contradictions' are only apparent and not real. 'Good and evil are not two things, but one, the difference being only in manifestation—one of degree and not of kind. Thus the same truth manifests—both in our relative error and knowledge, the same bliss manifests itself as good and evil; and the same real existence appears as both life and death'.

Marxists contend that the processes of nature follow their laws of the dialectic, though, as R.N. Carew Hunt

* R.N. Carew Hunt

muses, 'if this be so, it is strange that all the great scientific discoveries should have been made without apparent reference to it'.

Engles, borrowing a Hegelian illustration, shows how 'a grain of barley germinates and dies, and from it there arises a plant which is the negation of the grain. This plant grows, and finally produces a stalk at the end of which are further grains of barley. 'As soon as these are ripened the stalk dies and is in turn negated; and as a result of this negation of the negation, the original grain of barley is multiplied tenfold'—thereby supposedly demonstrating that a change negates a given state.

In contradistinction to this, Vivekananda holds that 'everything in the universe begins from certain rudiments, certain fine forms, and becomes grosser and grosser and again goes back to that fine form and subsides'. 'The relation of cause and effect is one of evolution—the one becomes the other, and so on. Sometimes the cause vanishes, as it were, and in its place leaves the effect'.

Neither Hegel nor Engels cares to explain how the grain and the plant, or for that matter the stalk and the grains of barley represent contradictions. The distinction appears to be wholly arbitary. On the other hand, by applying Swamiji's principle, we arrive at a reasonable explanation: the grain and the plant are not separate but one, in finer and grosser form.

'What does man see around him? Take a little plant. He puts a seed in the ground, and later, he finds a plant peep out, lift itself slowly above the ground, and grow till it becomes a gigantic tree. Then it dies, leaving only the seed. It completes the circle—it comes out of the seed, becomes the tree, and ends in the seed again. Look at a bird, how from the egg it springs, lives its life, and then dies, leaving other eggs, seeds of future birds. So with the animals, so with man...So with everything in nature by which we are surrounded. We know that the huge mountains are being worked upon by glaciers and rivers, which are slowly but surely pounding them and pulverising them into sand, that drifts away into the ocean where it settles down on its bed, layer after layer, becoming hard as rocks, once more to be heaped up into mountains of a future generation. Again they will be pounded and pulverised, and thus the course goes on. From sand rise these mountains; into sand they go'. '... destruction means, going back to the cause. If this table here is destroyed, it will go back to its cause, to those fine forms and particles which, combined, made this form which we call a table ... Therefore we learn that the effect is the same as the cause, not different. It is only in another form'.

Applying Newton's law, Professor Sorokin says, 'Definite movement in one direction is impossible because friction and shocks of external forces would disturb the movement and eventually change its direction. Through the gravitational forces, for instance, a linear movement becomes circular and elliptical'.

Though Marx gave a new meaning and a sequence to the broken pageantry of history, and though it is his ideas, more than any other factor, that have strengthened the working class all over the globe, his theory of progress, based on Hegel's dialectic, is linear—a conclusion which, behind its mask of science, seems distorted. A straight line, extended infinitely, curves into a circle, and if it is true that nature is uniform throughout—and as Vivekananda says, 'so far no human experience has contradicted it'—then Marx has been found badly wanting.

On the other hand, Swamiji comes out quite unscathed. 'All progress', he says, 'is a successive rise and fall', a standpoint with which Toynbee could not agree more.

'We learn that all these particular forms, which we call plants, animals, or men are being repeated ad infinitum, rising and falling', Vivekananda says. 'The seed produces the tree. The tree produces the seed, which again comes up as another tree, and so on and on. There is no end to it'. 'There is one fact more to learn about this rising and falling. The seed comes out of the tree. It does not immediately become a tree, but has a period of inactivity, or rather, a period of very fine unmanifested action. The seed has to work for some time beneath the soil. It breaks into pieces, degenerates as it were, and regeneration comes out of that degeneration.

'In the beginning, the whole of this universe has to work likewise for a period in that minute form, unseen and unmanifested, which is called chaos, and out of that comes a new projection. The whole period of one manifestation of this universe ... is, in Sanskrit, called a Kalpa or a Cycle'. 'Everything ... is proceeding in the same way, like breathing in and breathing out in the human body'..

Obviously, for Vivekananda, historical evolution follows the same rise-and-fall pattern. 'In the same country there will be different tides; at one time the full flood of materialistic idea prevails, and everything in this life—prosperity, the education which procures more pleasures, more food—will become glorious first and then that will degenerate. Along with the prosperity will rise to white heat all the inborn jealousies and hatred of the human race, and competition and merciless cruelty will be the watchword of the day. Then the people think that the whole scheme of life is a failure. And the world would be destroyed, were not spirituality to come to rescue and lend a helping hand to the sinking world. Then the world gets new hope and finds a new basis for a new building and another wave of spirituality comes, which in time, again declines. As a rule, spirituality brings a class of men who lay exclusive claim to the special powers of the world. The immediate effect is a reaction towards materialism ... Materialism comes as a rescue'.

'I am a Socialist', Vivekananda wrote in one of his letters, but there is little reason to suppose that he over worked out that point to anything resembling a wholeness. Like Marx he envisioned a classless society, and like Marx he exalted the proletariat and advocated the elimination of privilege. 'That is really the work before the world', he said. 'The difficulty is not that one body of men are more intelligent than another but whether this body of men, because they have the advantages of intelligence, should take away even physical enjoyments from those who do not possess this intelligence'.

That is stating it somewhat simplistically, of course, for intelligence may or may not be the most important factor, let alone the sole one, in deciding who holds the reins of power. Be that as it may, Vivekananda authored no economic tract, and his statements on the art of government are not clearly defined. Human knowledge in the modern world has cast its net so wide that it is unimaginable that a single person will be able to eat the whole catch and digest it. Specialization is the order of the day, and perhaps rightly so. Vivekananda gave religion the pride of place in his scheme of things, and his amours with political theory were brief and flirtatious. Yet he emphasised the all-pervading nature of genuine spirituality. 'The Vedanta as a religion must be intensely practical', he said. 'We must be able to carry it out in every part of our lives. And not only this, the fictitious differentiation between religion and the life of the world must vanish'. 'The ideals of religion must cover the whole field of life, they must enter into all our thoughts'. 'If a religion cannot help man wherever he may be, wherever he stands, it is not of much use'.

By implication, Vivekananda would seem to be a democrat:

'Differentiation is the sign of life'.

'Liberty is the first condition of growth'. 'To advance oneself towards freedom, physical, mental, and spiritual, and help others to do so is the prize of man'.

'It is more blessed in my opinion, even to go wrong by one's free will and intelligence than to be good as an automaton'.

'Destroy those social rules which stand in the way of unfoldment of this freedom and are therefore injurious'

'Can that be called a society which is formed by an aggregate of men, who are like lumps of clay, like lifeless machines, like heaped-up pebbles? How can such a society fare well? For in such a society all initiative, all inventive genius, all capacities of appreciation and discrimination are stifled to death'.

It is important to be able to follow the creative impulse, Vivekananda would say, for that is precisely what brings relish to life and makes life worth living. But freedom must not descend into licentiousness. 'Liberty does not mean the absence of obstacles in the path of misappropriation of other people's wealth etc. by you and me . . .'

There are unmistakable grounds for disenchantment with the prevalent version of Indian democracy, and one wonders what adjustments Vivekananda would have recommended had he been in our midst today. When Marx said that franchise only gave the people the right to decide 'once in every three or six years which member of the ruling class is to misrepresent them in Parliament', he came within a hair's breadth of describing conditions in present-day India. What can one expect from a system in which the typical M.L.A. or M.P. launches his political career with a lie—a false declaration to the effect that his election expenses have not exceeded the stipulated ceiling of Rs. 35,000? Chances are he will have spent not less than twenty times as much, possibly a great deal more. Company donations have been banned. Where do all the extra bags of money come from? Unaccounted sources, naturally. The result: an unholy alliance between black money and politics that serves as the backdrop for the parliamentary democracy of today's India—a plebiscitary democracy in which the people are helplessly dependant on the government for almost everything, and where the leaders go out to them at intervals to make false promises and seek their loyalty.

That the weaknesses of the present system need to be reviewed and viable alternatives found goes without saying, but what directions these might take is not within the purview of this book. There can be little doubt, however, that Vikekananda's first aim today would be to educate the masses. What he said almost a century ago is as pertinent now as it was then:

'The remedy now is the spread of education. My idea is to bring to the door of the meanest, the poorest, the noble ideas that the human race has developed both in and out of

India, and let them think for themselves'.

'The ideal of all education, all training should be man-making. Education is not the amount of information that is put into your brain and runs riot there, undigested, all your life. We must have life-building, man-making, character-making assimilation of ideas. If you have assimilated five ideas and made them your life and character, you have more education than any man who has got by heart a whole library... If education is identical with information, the libraries are the greatest sages in the world, and encyclopaedias are the Rishis'.

'I look upon religion as the innermost core of education'. 'What we want are Western Science coupled with Vedanta'. 'Every improvement in India requires first of all an upheaval in religion. ('The Indian mind is first religious, then anything else... The national ideals of India are renunciation and service. Intensify her in those channels, and the rest will take care of itself'). Before flooding India with socialistic or political ideas, first deluge the land with spiritual ideas... After preaching spiritual knowledge, along with it will come that secular knowledge and every other knowledge that you want; but if you attempt to get the secular knowledge without religion, I tell you plainly, vain is your attempt in India, it will never have a hold on the people'.

"Your duty at present is to go from one part of the country to another, from village to village, and make the people understand that mere sitting about idly won't do any more. Make them understand their real condition and say, 'O ye brothers, all arise! Awake! How much longer would you remain asleep?"

He himself discharged this 'duty' by setting up the Ramakrishna Mission, the last great religious and social movement of 19th century India, which has been singularly successful both in and outside India. It aims not only to open the hidden doors of spirituality in individuals, irrespective of caste, creed or colour, but also engages in a wide range of philanthropic work, including running schools, hospitals, and dispensaries, helping the blind, and rendering aid to the victims of natural calamities.

In one sense, the Mission may be said to be a monument to Vivekananda's organisational ability and his sympathetic concern for the plight of mankind: '... do you really feel for your brothers? Do you really feel that there is so much misery in the world, so much ignorance and superstition? Do you really feel that men are your brothers? Does this idea come into your whole being? Does it run with your blood? Does it tingle in your veins? Does it course through every nerve and filament of your body? Are you full of that idea of sympathy?'

However, to what extent institutionalism, which the creation of the Mission implies, is conducive to spiritual freedom and growth is another matter. In the phenomenal world, the ideal is always elusive.

There is another interesting angle from which the mystic views man's relationship with society.

All life is relationship. You may think of yourself as a separate ego in a bag of skin, but the very fact of your birth is the outcome of a relationship and the cause of others. The way you think and behave and the way you look are not all your own—heredity and environment have a good deal to do with them. Your covering of skin which you look upon as your physical boundary and beyond which the 'outside' world begins for you is in reality inseparable from that world: your skin has pores breathing air from that world, and nerve-ends relaying information from it. Here is a little story that will illustrate the point.

Randhir, being unemployed, used to spend his time at the library. On his way back he usually took a short cut through the lanes and by-lanes. But one Saturday evening it had been raining cats and dogs for over an hour. Randhir assumed that the smaller streets might be flooded, and so began walking down the main road. He had walked nearly half-way home when a car pulled up next to him and someone inside called out his name. Turning, he saw an old college friend for the first time in two years.

'Dev! What a surprise!' exclaimed Randhir.

'If you have the time, why don't you hop in?' said Dev.

So Randhir did. They shook hands and laughed and smacked one another and, in their excitement, tripped over each other's words. A five-minute drive and they were at a bar, re-living their good old days together.

Finally they came to the present, which they had but briefly touched upon till now. Dev had joined his father's advertising agency and was already earning a four-figure salary.

'How come you haven't landed a job? asked Dev. 'You were one of the bright ones in college, Ronny'.

'Well, I suppose, no luck and no strings to pull', answered Randhir.

'I say, exactly what kind of a job are you looking for.'

'I'm not an idealist any more, Dev. Anything will do, as long as its not downright roguery!'

'Bad scene, Ronny. Imagine a guy like you without a job!'

Randhir just shrugged. He wished they hadn't brought up the topic.

'Hey, I got an idea', said Dev, his face suddenly lighting up and regarding his friend's with close interest.

'Listening', said Randhir.

'I know this isn't your scene, Ronny, but you're a pretty pleasant-looking guy. We're looking for a suitable model for EXCLUSIVE cigarettes. Care to have a shot at it?'

Him a model? Well, Dev was right—it wasn't his scene. He pursed his lips and wondered how best to put across the fact that he thought it was a lousy idea.

'Take a good friend's advice, Ronny. Have a go at it. I'll be goddamned surprised if you don't make it'.

I . . . I'll think about it, Dev', is all that Randhir managed to say.

They exchanged phone-numbers, and Dev dropped Randhir home.

To cut a long story short, Randhir, spurred on by Dev, eventually paid a somewhat reluctant visit to the studio. Within two years he not only became one of the highest-paid models in the country, but was also offered character roles in movies. Soon he married a stage-actress, and eighteen months later they were blessed with a wonderful baby girl.

I.Q. question: What is the connection between the Saturday evening rain-fall in the first paragraph and the new-born child in the last?

Or consider this less pleasant story:

Mr. Roy had indigestion and turned grumpy with Mrs. Roy. This put Mrs. Roy into a bad mood. But instead of saying anything to her husband, she took it out on their son Bimal for coming back late from school. Bimal, unable to retaliate, kicked their pet dog Togo, at which Togo slouched out into the street and was run over by a speeding truck.

I.Q. question: What is the relationship between Mr. Roy's indigestion and Togo's death?

For the mystic, life's relationship have a further dimension—something in the nature of Mr. Cleve Backster's inherent 'primary perception' referred to earlier. Each person, so to speak, extends beyond his body, like the waves of a whirlpool spreading out wards in concentric patterns. Every person is, knowingly or not, a force in the world, an energy entity exerting either a positive or negative influence on his surroundings. If, for the sake of convenience and simplicity, I were to compare this influence with an odour, the question which would arise is: How do I emanate? Am I fragrant, or do I stink?

Either way, it sets off a chain reaction in the world around. In that sense, we are always acting upon and being acted upon by what is termed 'the outside world'—but which, the mystic will say, is simply an illusion because there is no 'outside' world but just one world, one universe, and you, I and we, are IT. We do not come 'into' the world; we come 'out of it' like fruits from a tree.

Because the mystic perceives this, he also perceives, to quote Ramana Maharshi, that 'self-reform automatically brings about social reform'. 'Stick to self-reform , he therefore advises, 'and social reform will take care of itself'.

Though certainly no mystic, G.B. Shaw had the wisdom to observe that 'the best reformers the world has ever seen are those who commence on themselves', and J. Lavater, expressing similar belief, has commented that 'he who reforms himself has done more towards reforming the public than a crowd of noisy, impotent patriots'.

So what does religion have to do with society? By reforming himself, the individual has already begun to reform society. He may be a grocer, a professor, or a politician. What matters is whether he is chasing the truth.

There is no greater responsibility than being a human being.

# Karma

ON 11TH MAY, 1812, the Prime Minister of England, Spencer Perceval, was shot dead in the House of Commons. An elderly gentleman living at Cornwall dreamt the entire incident thrice in succession and scene by scene, some eight or nine days before the assassination—a record that is well authenticated. That is not all. A few days before his death the Prime Minister himself had strong forebodings about the coming event, and promptly handed his will to his wife.

During the subsequent trial the assassin disclosed that he had no personal grievances against Mr Perceval. Though he was furious with the government, he had, in fact, intended to shoot somebody else, 'but Perceval appeared, and I felt I must kill someone'.

In our own time the far-famed Jean Dixon has gazed into her crystal-ball and accurately predicted the deaths of Mahatma Gandhi and President Kennedy.

Predestination?

Says Emerson: 'A little consideration of what takes place around us every day must show us that a higher law than that of our will regulates events'.

This law, Vivekananda avers, is the law of Karma. Karma means work. It 'also implies causation. Any work, any action, any thought that produces an effect is called a Karma. Thus the law of Karma means the law of causation, of inevitable cause and sequence'. 'Our Karma determines what we are and what we can assimilate. We are responsible for what we are; and whatever we wish ourselves to be, we have the power to make ourselves. If what we are now has been the result of our past actions, it certainly follows that whatever we wish to be in future can be produced by our present actions'. 'Man is not bound by any other laws excepting those which he makes for himself'.

As a Buddist verse puts it:

We are what we think,
having become what we thought.
Like the wheel that follows the cart-pulling ox,
Sorrow follows an evil thought.

and joy follows a pure thought,
like a shadow faithfully trailing a man.
We are what we think,
having become what we thought.

Why is one man's life cut off at the high noon of his career? Why does one man struggle to eke out a living while another has always lived in the lap of luxury? Why was A born blind and B with eyes? Why is X honest, intelligent, but unlucky, and Y dishonest, mediocre, but fortunate? Why? Isn't it unfair? Isn't it absurd?

No, says the law of Karma. As you sow so must you reap.

'But that's all stuff and nonsense!' you exclaim. 'What heinous crimes could a new-born have committed? How then, does he come into the world blind, or in poverty, or in a broken home?'

Let us proceed from the known to the unknown:

It is a well-established fact of modern psychology that the child is father of the man. What we are now is to a great extent the outcome of the experiences we underwent in our infancy. The circumstances of our youth moulded us and helped form the basis of our character. If that base was strong and sturdy, so are we now; if not, we still move on weak psychological foundations. And yet how many of us can recapture, however hard we may try, those formative occurrences of our now-nebulous childhood? They have sunk deep beneath the mind's surface into the zones of our subconscious, but, like the submerged nine-tenths of an iceberg, they are very much real. They are, indeed, the most substantial portion of our psychological make-up.

Similarly, by the law of Karma, the nature we are born

with is an extension, as it were, of the type of personality we died with in our previous life—for Karma suggests rebirth.

There are certain other questions.

Isn't it ironical that, though we generally assume that a good person, on dying, attains heavenly bliss, and yet we look upon his death as a tragedy? Tragedy for whom? For his dependants, may be, for the people he has left behind. But on what grounds do we conclude that it is a tragedy to the dead person.

And then, what is a good birth? I don't think there can be any objective criteria. To put it in a nut-shell, in our perspective, a good birth is that which offers ample scope for attaining the highest happiness and spiritual development. People often equate being born in a wealthy family with having had a good birth. But wealth is seldom a spiritual incentive. Nor is being born of spiritual-minded parents necessarily conducive to spiritual growth in the child, for as he grows up he may totally reject his parents' world.

There are individuals and individuals, and one man's meat is ever so often another man's poison. That is why it would be impossible to generalise on the karmic quality of any person's birth. For all one knows, being born blind may turn out to be a boon in disguise—Hellen Keller comes to mind—and being born in good shape in a comfortable home may ultimately deprive one of the struggle necessary to bring out one's spiritual best.

'Reincarnation depends on Karma', says Vivekananda. 'If a man accumulates Karma akin to his beastly nature, he will be drawn thereto'. 'People ... think it too horrible that man should come up from an animal. Why? What will be the end of these millions of animals? Are they nothing? I, we have a soul, so have they, and if they have none, neither have we. It is absurd to say that man alone has a soul, and the animals none. I have seen men worse than animals'.

Does that sound irrational? The question brings to mind Bernad Shaw's encounter with the famous Indian scientist

J.C. Bose in London. Shaw, a proud vegetarian, apparently squirmed in his boots as Bose revealed how raw carrots, on being pinched and pierced, emitted violent electrical signals corresponding to man's cries for help! Bose further demonstrated how a piece of sheet metal, plant fibre, and animal muscle reacted to outside stimuli in practically similar ways—the difference being not in kind but in degree.

'At a Royal Institute lecture in London, Sir J.C. Bose demonstrated the dying condition of a piece of tin by the application of poison and then revived it by rendering medical aid ... He ended his lecture with a peroration ... that this Unity in life throughout all objects in this Universe was found by the Ancient Sages of India—who beholds this, the eternal truth will belong to him only.

'As the peroration ended a great applause greeted him. Sir Robert Austen, the greatest authority on metals, was besides himself with joy. He said, "I have all my life studied the properties of metals. I am happy to think that they have life ..."'

(From JAGADISH CHANDRA BOSE: A BIOGRAPHY, by Manoranjan Gupta; Bharatiya Vidya Bhavan, Bombay)

Professor Max Planck says, 'Consciousness I regard as fundamental. I regard matter as derivative from consciousness. We cannot get behind consciousness. Everything that we talk about, everything that we regard as existing, postulates consciousness'.

Transmigration is familiar in Greek thought: in Pythagoras, Empedocles ('Thus in former lives, I have been a boy and a girl, a bush and a bird and a fish without speech in the depths of the sea'), and Plato, who held that 'the character the soul had acquired by deeds and experiences would decide whether it should rise or sink lower in the next birth. Emancipation would come only through self-development'.

However, to Vivekananda, as to all Vedantists, the term 'transmigration' would refer not to the soul, but to the 'mind-stuff'—the subtle, condensed mental essence of a person—for the soul is omnipresent. 'The Atman (soul) never comes nor goes, is never born nor dies. It is nature moving before the Atman, and the reflection of this motion is on the Atman'. 'There is but one Soul in the universe, not two.

'It neither comes nor goes. It is neither born, nor dies, nor reincarnates. How can It die? Where can It go? All this universe is the reflection of that One Eternal Being, the Atman, and as the reflection falls upon good or bad reflectors, so good or bad images are cast up. Thus in the murderer, the reflector is bad and not the self. In the saint the reflector is pure. The self—the Atman—is by Its own nature pure. It is the same, the one Existence of the universe that is reflecting Itself from the lowest worm to the highest and most perfect being. The whole of this universe is one Unity, one Existence, physically, mentally, morally and spiritually.'

Everything,—expect a dead, and therefore soulless body—is in a state of vibration. Only the vibrations are higher or lower. Since cosmic energy is inherently dynamic, and since all forms of matter are modifications of this 'Prana' or primal energy, whatever exists in the universe vibrates within this 'Prana'. It was Pythagoras, if I remember correctly, who first told us that everything in this world, both the visible and the invisible, vibrates. The grosser the body is, of course, the lower the rate of vibration—and when we come to the grossest we tend to think that they have no vibrations at all. But that is not so. Their frequencies are so low that we are, under normal conditions, insensitive to them altogether.

What Vivekananda refers to as the 'mind-stuff' is the concentrated essence of a person's mental processes. From the Vedantic standpoint this is nature ('prakriti') or matter in its most subtle form and at its highest possible frequency. But inspite of its refinement it is doomed to eventual destruction like all other matter. This lingers on after (bodily) death and transmigrates', into an appropriate receptacle.

At this point the inevitable question is: How is mind matter?

There's an old crack which goes, 'What is mind?—Doesn't matter! What is matter?—Never mind!', but let's pass over the joke and ask those very questions, for they are relevant to our purpose.

What is perception and what role does the mind play in it?

Vivekananda gives the following explanations:

'I am looking at you. How many things are necessary for this vision? First, the eyes. For if I am perfect in every other way, and yet have no eyes, I shall not be able to see you. Secondly, the real organs of vision. For the eyes are not the organs. They are but the instruments of vision, and behind them is the real organ, the nerve centre in the brain. If that centre be injured, a man may have the clearest pair of eyes, yet he will not be able to see anything. So it is necessary that this centre, or the real organ, be there. Thus, with all our senses. The external ear is but the instrument for carrying the vibration of sound inward to the centre. Yet, that is not sufficient. Suppose in your library you are intently reading a book, and the clock strikes, yet you do not hear it. The sound is there, the pulsations in the air are there, the ear and the centre are also there, and these vibrations have been carried through the ear to the centre, and yet you do not hear it. What is wanting? The mind is not there. Thus we see that the third thing necessary is that the mind must be there ... The mind, too, is only the carrier; it has to carry the sensation still forward, and present it to the intellect. The intellect is the determining faculty and decides upon what is brought to it. Still this is not sufficient. The intellect must carry it forward and present the whole thing before the ruler in the body, the human soul, the king on the throne ...

'The instruments are in the external body, the gross body of man; but the mind and the intellect are not. They are in what is called in Hindu philosophy the finer body, and what in Christian theology you read of as the spiritual body of man; finer, very much finer than the body, and yet not the soul. The soul is beyond them all'.

For our purposes, however, we shall consider the

intellect as part of the mind. Patanjali, the compiler of the famous Yoga aphorisms, divides the 'chitta' (mind) into 'manas, buddhi, and ahamkar' (the recording and discriminating faculties, and the ego-sense respectively). He gives an example. Suppose a bull is on the verge of attacking him. The 'manas' says: a large animate object is quickly approaching; the 'buddhi' decides: it is a bull. It is angry. It is going to charge. The 'ahamkar' declares: it wants to attack me, Patanjali. It is I, Patanjali, who sees the bull. It is I who am frightened. It is I who am going to beat it'.

It is a fundamental characteristic of matter, or nature, both organic and inorganic, to be in a perpetual state of flux. We have already had this exemplified in the previous chapter, and it is precisely this principle the Greek philosopher Heraclitus was bringing to our notice when he declared that you could not jump into the same river twice. The mental functions follow the same pattern of continual change. Vivekananda compares it to 'the maddened monkey—incessantly active by its own nature'. Like all matter, thoughts are born, they grow, and they die. Thus 'both body and mind belong to nature and must obey nature's laws'. 'Whatever has form must break sometime or other. There cannot be any form unless it is the result of force and matter; and all combinations must dissolve'. 'What do we mean by destruction? Destruction is disintegration of the materials out of which anything is composed. If this glass is broken into pieces the materials will disintegrate, and that will be the destruction of the glass. Disintegration of particles is what we mean by destruction.

Another thing: can the mind feel, think? Obviously not, if it is matter. Matter is not intelligent. Yet the mind does seem to behave as if it were intelligent. How, then, do we resolve this puzzle?

'Soul...is the manufacturer of thought, but not thought itself; it is the manufacturer of the body, but not the body. Why so? We see that the body cannot be the soul. Why not? Because it is not intelligent. A corpse is not intelligent, nor a piece of meat in a butcher's shop. What do we mean by intelligence? Reactive power'.

The soul, then, is the supreme background through which the mind interprets and coordinates all its experiences. It is, as it were, the screen against which the mind throws its images. But there is still another way by which we arrive at the conclusion that there must be something beyond the mind:

'By dint of hard work, thoughts may be silenced altogether. If thoughts were the real man, as soon as thought ceases, he ought to die. Thought ceases in meditation; even the mind's elements are quite quiet. Blood circulation stops. His breath stops, but he is not dead. If thought were he, the whole thing ought to go, but they find it does not. That is practical proof'. (e.g. the trances of Ramakrishna).

The Soul, therefore, is not subject to the laws of nature. It exists in stillness, consciously and passively. If it can exist in stillness, it cannot be composed of particles, because particles are inherently mobile. It would automatically follow 'that nothing that is not composed of particles can be destroyed, can ever be disintegrated. The soul is not composed of any materials. It is unity indivisible. Therefore, it must be indestructible. For the same reasons it must also be without any beginning. So the soul is without any beginning and end', since what has a beginning must have an end.

Argument: If all is Brahman, as Vivekananda contends, then, 'body' is Brahman; 'mind' is Brahman; nature is Brahman. And Brahman is Consciousness, Quiescence. But matter is dull, insensible, ever-moving. So the theory goes phut.

Answer: Many consider this the vulnerable point of the Advaita Vedanta philosophy. A friend of mine remarked that it was like a beautiful lady with a missing front tooth— and this, of course, deprived her of some of her appeal. When I gave him Vivekananda's explanation, he quipped that Vivekananda had filled up the awkward gap with a false tooth! But that is good jest and bad logic, as the matter at hand is purely abstract for us ordinary mortals, and, as such, not a subject we can pass final judgement on.

Vivekananda says, 'We see this world with the five senses, but if we had another sense, we would see in it something more. If we had yet another sense, it would appear as something still different. It has, therefore, no real existence; it has no unchangeable, immovable, infinite existence. Nor can it be called non existence, seeing that it exists, and we have to work in and through it. It is a mixture of existence and non-existence'.

Only the eternal, then, is real. The rest is Maya—a dream, a mirage, an illusion. The body is Maya and the mind is Maya. The entire phenomenal world is Maya. Vivekananda describes man thus; 'Man, Infinite man, dreaming finite dreams!' It is like trying to grasp a sunbeam; it is like trying to get hold of an object by clutching at its shadow. Or to use Shankara's famous example, it is like seeing a rope in the dark and mistaking it for a snake.

But a dream is true to the dreamer while he is dreaming. In that sense, at least, it is not unreal. But neither can it be called real, seeing that it does not exist in actuality. Hence Maya is neither real nor unreal.

You ask: Can you prove that all phenomena is Maya?

That is not a valid question, Vivekananda would say. You are living within Maya, so you have no right to ask that question. If you are living in stink, after a time you stop feling the stink any more; but were you to step out into a fresher environment and return, you would get the stink once again. Similarly, it is only when you have woken up that you know that you had dreamt. So, wake up! Transcend your senses! Look at reality as it is, not as it appears to be! 'The excuse of our ignorance is a kind of mist that has come between us and the truth', he says. He quotes from the Upanishads: 'Know nature to be Maya and the Ruler of this Maya is the Lord Himself'.

A Hindu sage has thus tried to express the ineffable nature of Brahman:

'He stays, yet wanders far from hence,
He reposes, yet strays everywhere around,

The movement hither and thither of the God,
Who could understand besides me?'

Ramakrishna once stated that in God all contradictions
meet, and are resolved. Such statements are apt to strike
one as incomprehensible. Yet are not such seeming contradictions an empirical fact of our everyday experience?
When waves from the sea roll down, do we not get the
impression that the water is flowing? And yet, when you
watch objects floating in the sea, do you notice any
forward or backward movement? They bob up and down
with the waves, but they all remain in the same place.
There is only 'wave' motion, there is only vibration.

We have seen that everything in the universe vibrates
within the primal energy, called, 'Prana' in Sanskrit. Why,
then, does a corpse not vibrate? Because it is not real,
because the soul—which alone is real—has left the body.

Is the soul, then, a part of God? No, it is God Itself:

'Can Infinity have parts? What is meant by parts of
Infinity? If you reason it out, you will find that it is
impossible. Infinity cannot be divided, it always remains
infinite. If it could be divided, each part would be infinite.
And there cannot be two Infinities. Suppose there were,
one would limit the other, and both would be finite.
Infinity can only be one, undivided. Thus the conclusion
will be reached that the Infinite is one and not many, and
that one Infinite Soul is reflecting itself through thousands
and thousands of mirrors, appearing as many different
souls. It is the same Infinite Soul, which is the background
of the universe, that we call God. The same Infinite Soul
also is the background of the human mind which we call
the human soul'.

'We become identified with our emotions, but when
this inner vision, this introspection awakens in us, we
discover our troubles in their subtlest form and, at the
same time, we can say, 'I am not my troubles; I am not my
anger, I am separate from it and I am separate from these
emotions and all these tendencies. I am a free soul.' "

And so it is that Vivekananda calls upon us to 'say not

man is a sinner. Tell him that he is a God'. "Go and preach to all: 'Arise, awake, sleep no more; within each of you there is the power to remove all wants and miseries. Believe this, and that power will be manifested' ".

The Chinese philosopher-mystic Lao Tse urges us to 'get into harmony with the Tao—the Great Spirit in things', for by so doing 'you will be unconsciously impelled to right action'.

At the age of seventy Confucious declared: 'At fifteen I began to be seriously interested in study. At thirty I had formed my character. At fifty I knew the will of heaven. At sixty nothing that I heard disturbed me. At seventy I could let my thoughts wander without trespassing the moral law'.

The mind, being matter, is no more sentient than a corpse. But it has a more intimate relationship with the soul than the body. Their alliance has been deftly explained through an analogy. Kovoor T. Behanan mentions the following story: 'Two men, one lame and the other blind, were, each in his own way, seeking a way through the jungle. They agreed to fulfil their duties by mutual cooperation. The lame man climbed on the shoulders of the blind man and by following the former's directions both of them reached their destinations. The soul could see but not 'move'—like the lame man. Prakriti (Nature) could move, but not see—like the blind man. When they reached their destination, there was a separation. Prakriti ceased to act, for its work was done, and purusha (the soul), having reached the journey's end, was free forever after'.

Vivekananda says that 'each work we do, each thought we think, produces an impression, called in Sanskrit Samskara, upon the mind, and the sum total of these impressions becomes the tremendous force which is called character. The character of a man is what he has created for himself...The sum total of the Samskara is the force which gives a man the next direction after death. A man dies; the body falls away and goes back to the elements; but the Samskara remain, adhering to the mind which, being made of fine material, does not dissolve, because the finer the material, the more persistent it is. But the mind also dissolves in the long run, and that is what we are struggling for. In this connection, the best illustration that comes to my mind is that of the whirlwind. Different currents of air coming from different directions meet, and at the meeting point become united and go on rotating; as they rotate they form a body of dust, drawing in bits of paper, straw, etc. at one place, only to drop them and go on to another, and so go on rotating, raising and forming bodies out of the materials which are before them. Even so the forces, called Prana in Sanskrit, come together and form the body and the mind out of matter, and move on until the body falls down, when they raise other materials, to make another body, and when this falls, another arises, and thus the process goes on. Force cannot travel without matter. So when the body falls down, the mind-stuff remains, Prana in the form of Samskaras acting on it, and then it goes on to another point, raises up another whirl from fresh materials, and begins another motion; and so it travels from place to place until the force is all spent; and then it falls down, ended. So when the mind will end, be broken to pieces entirely, without leaving any Samskara, we shall be entirely free, and until that time we are in bondage; until then the Atman is covered by the whirl of the mind, and imagines it is being taken from place to place. When the whirl falls down, the Atman finds that it is all-pervading'.

The Atman is the Holy Ghost of the Biblical Trinity, and the purpose of all religions is to make men heark 'the still small voice' within them, 'to be filled with the Holy Spirit' so that 'Thy will be done on earth as it is in Heaven'.

How is this to be achieved? Surely, not by merely wishing it: 'By their fruits ye shall know them...Not every-one that saith unto me, Lord, Lord, shall enter the king-dom of heaven; but he that doeth the will of my Father who is in heaven'. 'Marvel not that I said unto thee, ye must be born again'.

This spiritual rebirth 'is not for the glutton', says the Gita, 'or one who fasts too much; it is not for the sleep-heavy or the sleepless; it is only for the moderate in eating and resting, in sleeping and working'. 'Abandoning the fruits of work, the balanced mind attains tranquillity; but the unsteady mind, motivated by greed, is trapped in its own reward'.

I take it that the last statement implies a qualification, for the idea of working just for nothing is abstruse and, indeed, meaningless. If you have nothing to work for, you will not work—it is as simple as that. Even if you voluntarily submit yourself to the worst form of drudgery, you will not, as surely as night follows day, do so without first hitching yourself to some moral, emotional, philosophic, or practical end. You can psychologically abandon the material and cruder rewards of work (like prosperity or fame, which are ephemeral, arouse the protective instinct, lead to feelings of insecurity, and are self-defeating because they do not bring you the ultimate gain you worked for, namely, happiness) only in the hope of reaping subtler and stabler harvests. You can work out of love for your job, for instance, in which case, since your happiness is analogous to your work, you spare yourself the agony of waiting for your reward. Since your work is itself your reward, your rewards are immediate every time you get down to work. Then work, in fact, is 'play'. Vivekananda or, for that matter, any great religious teacher, would advise you, of course, not to lean on your job psychologically, to develop the capacity to 'attach or detach any minute' and thereby be inwardly independent. But, all said and done, this exhortation too has a motive force—the promise of enlightenment.

Krishna tells Arjuna, 'I have no duty, nothing not attained and nothing to attain, yet even I persist in work'. But for all that, don't the Hindu scriptures conceive of creation as God's play? ('In play is the creation spread out, in play it is established') This is, after all, a kind of psychological motivation. It is something like the sense of flow and fulfilment that comes from a creative act or from doing something one has a natural affinity to. A poet under inspiration, a sportsman who has found his rhythm during the course of a game, or a lover who has made love with his loved one will know what it means to do something for its own sake. The point is whether we can extend this feeling to cover the gamut of our activities—from brushing our teeth in the morning to untying our shoe-laces at night. Is it possible to put the whole of our being into whatever we do, to give it our whole attention so that there is no sense of being isolated, separate, from what we do? If it is, then that is the end of all alienation, of frustration, of inefficiency, of egotism. Then we are like God, whose nature it is to 'play', like it is the sun's to shine.

Perhaps Vivekananda stretches the point a little too far when he insists that though he has 'read many arguments against the Bhagavad-Gita, and many have said that without motives you cannot work', their viewpoints are prejudiced because 'they have never seen unselfish work except under the influence of fanaticism, and therefore they speak in that way'. Man may reach the state of Godhood and then work for work's sake, without desire, but what is natural today may be nevertheless, yesterday's effort.

Vivekananda claims that Buddha 'is the one man who ever carried this (Karma Yoga or 'the attaining through unselfish work of that freedom which is the goal of all human nature') into perfect practice. All the prophets of the world, except Buddha, had external motives to move them to unselfish action. The prophets of the world, with this single exception, may be divided into two sets—one set holding that they are incarnations of God come down on earth, and the other holding that they are only messengers from God; and both draw their impetus for work from outside, accept reward from outside, however highly spiritual may be the language they use. But Buddha is the only prophet who said, "I do not care to know your various theories about God. What is the use of discussing all the subtle doctrines about the soul? Do good and be good. And this will take you to freedom and to whatever truth there is". He was, in the conduct of his life, absolutely without personal motives ...'

What reduced the voltage of Vivekananda's brilliance in this instance would be difficult to surmise, but any wary reader is bound to note the inconsistency of the previous quotation; for 'And this will take you to freedom and to whatever truth there is' is, if anything, a stimulus to adopt a certain morality: a morality that is supremely bene-volent, certainly, but one that is also fastened to an enlightened self-interest. And if Buddha's motivation did not come from 'outside', it nevertheless did arise from 'inside'.

The aspiring Karma Yogi, therefore, is unselfish not because he is indifferent to himself, but because it pleases him to be unselfish. He measures his life not by palpable yardsticks, but by philosophic ones. It serves his purpose to "never say 'Mine'". To him 'the very reason of nature's existence is for the education of the soul; it has no other meaning; it is there because the soul must have knowledge and through knowledge free itself'. 'Our duty to others means helping others, doing good to the world. Why should we do good to the world? Apparently to help the world, but really to help ourselves'. 'The main effect of work done for others is to purify ourselves'. 'We cannot add happiness to this world; similarly we cannot add pain to it either. The sum total of the energies of pleasure and pain displayed here on earth will be the same throughout. We just push it from this side to the other side, and from that side to this; but it will remain the same, because to remain so is its very nature'. 'This world is like a dog's curly tail, and people have been striving to straighten it out for hundreds of years; but when they let it go, it has curled up again. How could it be otherwise?' 'This world will always continue to be a mixture of good and evil. Our duty is to sympathise with the weak and to love even the wrong-doer. The world is a grand moral gymnasium wherein we have all to take exercise so as to become stronger and stronger spiritually'.

The religious man of action views work as a means 'to bring out the power of the mind . . . to wake up the soul.'

To him 'the different works are like blows to bring them out, to cause these giants to wake up.' 'Suppose there is a ball in this room, and we each have a mallet in our hands and begin to strike the ball, giving it hundreds of blows, driving it from point to point, until at last it flies out of the room. With what force and in what direction will it go out? These will be determined by the forces that have been acting upon it all through the room. All the different blows that have been given will have their effects. Each one of our actions, mental and physical, is such a blow. The human mind is a ball which is being hit. We are being hit about the room of the world all the time, and the passage out of it is determined by the force of all these blows.

The idea of overcoming the mind is an intriguing thought. What does it really mean—getting beyond the mind? Is it at all possible?

Have you not sometimes 'lost yourself' in some act or the other?—in listening to music, for instance, or in the process of reading an interesting book? Then there is no actor and no action; there is only 'acting'. You, the subject, by identifying yourself with the object, have melted into the latter, as it were, much as a spoonful of sugar might dissolve in a cup of hot tea. It is the absence of your self-consciousness while absorbed in the act that constitutes your happiness. At the time you are, naturally, not aware that you are happy—you are too absorbed just 'acting'. It is only the memory of that 'acting' that may later prompt you to remark, 'I was happy.' The memory is distinct from the original source of happiness, though undoubtedly a remembrance might evoke sensations that are pleasant in their own right. But this kind of 'acting' is only possible because, at least for the kind of 'acting' is only possible because, at least for the moment, you have got the better of your ego and lost your sense of 'I' and 'mine'—the burden of individuality that characterises the mind and circumscribes its motion. The mind is an accumulation of conscious, subconscious, and unconscious memories that reflects your sensate values (your intellectual conditioning, your acquisitive and self-protective instincts, etc.) and makes you see reality not as it is, but as it apears to be. Thus a superstitious man discerns a stump of tree in the dark and mistakes it for a ghost; a thief fancies it to be a policeman; and a fellow on a proposed rendezvous greets it as if it were his companion!

We are doing this all the time. We look at the world through the bias of our minds and fail to see reality as it is. We have been taught to believe that Mr. G.H. is a profound man and that white skin is more beautiful than black. So in whatever Mr G.H. says we read meanings that do not exist, and beautiful black people pass us by unnoticed. Or we 'know' that Mr X is quarrelsome—and with this 'knowledge' we avoid him like the plague. We typecast reality, but reality is ever-flowing, dynamic.

So we see that the mind's images are essentially false. They are subjective, whereas reality is objective. Non-attachment essentially consists of stripping the mind bare and permitting it to follow the dictates of the soul, which is the true and unbiased perceiver, the 'mine of infinite knowledge':

"No knowledge comes from outside; it is all inside. What we say a man 'knows', should, in strict psychological language, be what he 'discovers' or 'unveils', what a man 'learns' is really what he 'discovers' by taking the cover off his own soul, which is a mine of infinite knowledge. We say Newton discovered gravitation. Was it sitting anywhere in a corner waiting for him? It was in his own mind; the time came and he found it out". '... the advance of knowledge is made by the advance of this process of uncovering. The man from whom this veil is being lifted is the more knowing man; the man upon whom it lies thick is ignorant; and the man from whom it has entirely gone is all-knowing, omniscient. There have been omniscient men, and, I believe, there will be yet; and that there will be myriads of them in the cycles to come. Like fire in a piece of flint, knowledge exists in the mind; suggestion is the friction which brings it out'.

'Why does man go out to look for a God? ... It is your own heart beating, and you did not know, you were mistaking it for something external. He, nearest of the near, my own self, the reality of my own life, my body and my soul—I am Thee and Thou art Me'.

Kant came to the decision that no knowledge that does not refer to phenomena can be acquired except by revelation through inspiration. Vivekananda would add that this 'revelation' is accessible to all—the 'peace and knowledge', as Walt Whitman puts it, 'that pass all the argument of the earth':

'I believe in you, my Soul ...
Loaf with me on the grass, loose the stop from your
    throat,
Only the lull I like, the hum of your valved voice.
I mind how once we lay, such a transparent summer
    morning.
Swiftly arose and spread around me the peace and
    knowledge that pass all the argument of the earth,
And I know that the hand of God is the promise of
    my own,
And I know that the spirit of God is the brother of
    my own,
And that all the men ever born are also my brothers
    and the women my sisters and lovers,
And that a kelson of the creation is love'.

"The guiding motive of mankind', Vivekananda says, "should be charity towards men, charity towards all animals. But these are all various expressions of that one eternal truth that 'I am the universe; this universe is one'. Or else, where is the reason? Why should I do good to my fellowmen? Why should I do good to others? What compels me? It is sympathy, the feeling of sameness everywhere. The hardest hearts feel sympathy for other beings sometimes. Even the man who gets frightened if he is is told that this assumed individuality is really a delusion, that it is ignoble to try to cling to this apparent individuality, that very man will tell you that extreme self-abnegation is the centre of all morality.

And what is perfect self-abnegation? It means the abnegation of this apparent self, the abnegation of all selfishness. The idea of 'me and mine' is the result of past superstition, and the more this present self passes away, the more the real self becomes manifest. This is true self-abnegation, the centre, the basis, the gist of all moral teaching".

"So long as there is desire or want, it is a sure sign that there is imperfection. A perfect, free being cannot have any desire. God cannot want anything. If He desires, He cannot be God. He will be imperfect. So all the talk of God desiring this and that, becoming angry and pleased by turns is babies' talk, but means nothing. Therefore it has been taught by all teachers: 'Desire nothing, give up all desires and be perfectly satisfied'".

"The wall has no desires, so neither has the perfect man. But the wall is not sentient enough to desire, while for the perfect man there is nothing to desire. There are idiots who have no desires in this world, because their brain is imperfect. At the same time, the highest state is when we have no desires, but the two are opposite poles of the same existence. One is near the animal, and other near to God".

A mother wants to possess her son. She deludes herself into believing that this is an expression of the highest love. But it is only a camouflaged effect of psychological insecurity. Love is democratic. It gives without reflecting the giver. As soon as a demand is made, love degenerates into trade. Love knows no conditions, it is not a contract, it cannot be bound. Binding is a weakness, a limitation, an attribute of the finite, at odds with the infinite aspirations of religion. The mother who is willing to be fond of her child only so long as it echoes her wishes and accomplishes her desires loves not the child, but herself. She is tied up by her own wants and seeks to be released by another. Society has given her the whip-hand over her child, and she uses it, unknowingly though, as a slave. She is her own slave, and also makes slaves of others. This cannot be love, for love is freedom.

"The man who gives up living in houses, wearing fine clothes, and eating good food, and goes into the desert, may be a most attached person. His only possession, his own body, may become everything to him; and as he lives he will be simply struggling for the sake of his body. Non-attachment does not mean anything that we may do in relation to our external body, it is all in the mind. The binding link of 'I and mine' is in the mind. If we have not this link with the body and with the things of the senses, we are non-attached wherever and whatever we may be. A man may be on a throne and perfectly non-attached; another man may be in rags and still very much attached. First we have to attain this state of non-attachment, and then to work incessantly. Karma-Yoga gives us the method that will help us in giving up all attachment, though it is indeed very hard'.

There is the story of the two monks who were walking down a road when they came across a pool of water. There was a beautiful young woman on the other side, wanting to cross over, but helplessly looking at the pool.

The monks waded through the water, and one of them, seeing her plight, volunteered to lend her a helping hand. Actually, it was a little more than a helping hand, for he lifted her bodily and carried her across the water.

That done, the two monks silently resumed their journey.

Much later, as they were taking dinner, one of the monks suddenly asked, 'Didn't you feel ashamed holding that woman, being a monk?'

His companion answered, 'It's true I carried the woman across. But that's where I left her, while you've been holding onto her all this while!'

So it is not so much our outward actions as our attitude to things that decides whether we are 'attached' or not.

Non-attachment is disinterestedness, not uninterestedness. It is not sluggishness, but intense activity. In this context it is instructive to note that the Vedantists hold that Prana (the primal energy), of which all matter is a manifestation in one form or the other, comprises the

three varieties of 'gunas' or cosmic forces—Sattva,
Rajas, and Tamas. These 'gunas' correspond to the
colours white, red, and black respectively. 'These as
manifested in the physical world are what we may call
equilibrium, activity, and inertness. Tamas is typified as
darkness or inactivity; Rajas is activity, expressed as
attraction or repulsion; and Sattva is the equilibrium of the
two'. In inert matter, as a piece of rock, Tamas reigns
supreme, but the vestige of Rajas in it makes it possible to
change.

'In every man there are these forces. Sometimes Tamas
prevails. We become lazy, we cannot move, we are
inactive, bound down by certain ideas or by mere
dullness. At another time activity prevails, and at still
other times the calm balancing of both. Again, in different
men, one of these forces is generally predominant. The
characteristic of one man is inactivity, dullness and
laziness; that of another activity, power, manifestation of
energy; and in still another we find the sweetness,
calmness, and gentleness which are due to the balancing of
both action and inaction'.

Karma Yoga aims at making every man a Sattvika. Says
Krishna to Arjuna: 'The discipline that organises the
mind, the life-breath, and the senses, is Sattvika'. 'Action
performed without love or hate, without desire for its fruit,
is Sattvika'. 'The mind that knows the difference between
work and renunciation, right and wrong, bondage and
liberation, fear and fearlessness, is Sattvika'.

Corroborating the same idea, Vivekananda urges us to
'work like a master and not as a slave; work incessantly,
but do not do slave's work. Do you not see how everybody
works? Nobody can be altogether at rest; ninety-nine per
cent of mankind work like slaves, and the result is misery;
it is all selfish work. Work through freedom! Work
through love! The word 'love' is very difficult to understand; love never comes until there is freedom. There is no
true love possible in the slave. If you buy a slave and tie
him down in chains and make him work for you, he will
work like a drudge, but there will be no love in him. So

when we ourselves work for the things of the world as slaves, there can be no love in us, and our work is not true work...Selfish work is slave's work, and here is a test. Every act of love brings happiness; there is no act of love which does not bring peace and blessedness as its reaction'.

'There is...one great danger in human nature, viz. that man never examines himself...When we begin to work earnestly in the world, nature gives us blows right and left and soon enables us to find out our position. No man can long occupy satisfactorily a position for which he is not fit. There is no use in grumbling against nature's adjustment. He who does the lower work is not therefore a lower man. No man is to be judged by the mere nature of his duties, but all should be judged by the manner in which they perform them'.

Here again crops up the necessity of economic better-ment. A man should be able to work in an environment where he can more or less be his own true self; where he can put heart and soul into his job without worrying about making both ends meet. The more we can 'get into' our job, the more we can step out from the constrictions of our ego, and the more satisfaction we can derive from our work. At the same time, the quality of our work will be so much the better, because, as Vivekananda has it, 'the powers of the mind are like eyes of dissipated light; when they are concentrated they illumine'.

Dr. Suzuki, in a translated volume called 'The Zen Doctine of No-Mind' relates an anecdote throwing light on the technique of realisation—a technique that, as you will notice, is remarkably similar to the Karma Yogi's:

A Vinaya master called Yuan came to Tai-chu Hui-hai and asked, 'When disciplining oneself in the Tao, is there any special way of doing it?'

Hui-hai: Yes, there is.

Yuan   : What is that?

Hui-hai: When hungry one eats, when tired one sleeps.

Yuan   : That is what other people do; is their way the same as yours?

Hui-hai: Not the same.

Yuan  : Why not?

Hui-hai: When they eat, they do not just eat, they
          conjure up all kinds of imagination; when they
          sleep, they do not just sleep, they are given up
          to varieties of idle thoughts. That is why their
          way is not my way .

But is this practical? A thousand stray thoughts in my
mind are constantly battling for supremacy—sometimes
this one gains ascendancy and sometimes that. And they
have a habit of popping up at the oddest of times, catching
me totally unawares. How am I to overcome them? Like
Arjuna, I feel like sayig: 'The mind, Krishna, is powerful,
fickle, violent and uncontrollable. Harnessing the mind is
like harnessing the wind'.

I know Krishna's answer, but if does not seem the
perfect reply: 'The mind indeed is all that you say. Arjuna,
but determination helps, and renunciation curbs it'. In a
piece of doggerel, Tennyson says much the same thing:

O well for him whose will is strong
He will not have to suffer long.

Vivekananda is more realistic. True, he says, there's
nothing like a strong will. There's nothing you cannot do
with a will that is strong. How right Napoleon was!
Indeed, 'impossible' is a word to be found only in the
dictionary of fools. But take it easy! Don't overstrain your
will. Don't take more into your mouth than you can chew.
Go about it in a pragmatic way. See you don't end up
worse than you began. Don't overdo it, or it might just
boomerang! Be reasonable with yourself.

If Truth is in me, as the wisdom of the sages has it, then
surely I can discover it by myself. I don't know how long
or what precise form it will take, but what I do know of
faith is that It is there; and that to get at it, I must proceed
at my own pace. And because institutionalized religions,
whichever they may be, do not make sufficient allowances
for differences between individuals, I also know that they

cannot lead me to it. Perhaps some others can show me the way, but I have to get there by myself, using my own resources, such as they are. If my WILL TO TRUTH is strong enough, that itself will be my primary asset. There will be failures and disappointments, no doubt, as there have always been in the past. There will be traumatic moments of doubt and uncertainty...and much else that is difficult to put up with. But as long as my urge to know is genuine and deep enough not to be lured away by distractions, then I shall certainly find my way again sooner or later, however often I might lose it. As the American psychic Edgar Cayce put it, 'As ye apply, ye are given the next step'.

It's like the old story of the great sinner who, wanting desperately to reform, is told by a Rishi to chant the name of Lord Rama. But so steeped is he in sin that, try as he will, he can only manage to utter the name of the devil, Mara. And as he retires to the seclusion of the mountains and, with exemplary single-minded devotion, repeats the name over and over again, 'Mara' gradually transforms itself to 'Rama' and purges him clean.
His very will to good leads him to The Way.
   Says a Buddhist maxim:

> You are your own refuge;
> there is no other refuge.
> This refuge is hard to achieve.
> One's self is the lord of oneself;
> there is no other lord.
> This lord is difficult to conquer'.

And two celebrated quotations from the Dhammapada, a collection of sayings attributed to the Buddha, elaborates on The Way thus: 'Vigilance is the way of immortality. Heedlessness is the way of death. Those that are vigilant do not die. Those that are heedless are already as though dead'. 'By diligent attention, by reflection, by temperance, by self-mastery, the man of understanding makes for himself an island no flood can overwhelm'.

The greater the will to Truth, the more will such qualities manifest themselves in an individual. Nonetheless, the will to Truth is obviously not something that is equally distributed among individuals. In fact, we can risk the generalisation that the will to power is predominant in most people, with the will to pleasure possibly a close second. After all, what we will, too, is not independent of our karma. Therefore, to know ourselves is important, for without knowing ourselves it is impossible for us to ascertain what we are capable of and what we aren't and thus, to take accurate decisions in relation to our lives. Though all of us are similar, each of us is unique, and the diversity of our nature does not make us amendable to steam-roller generalizations.

What does all this imply? For one obsessed with power, for instance, it may be immensely more sensible to work out this obsession before setting out on other pursuits. For until this obsession is worked out, he will only be wasting his time in pursuing other goals. And that too at considerable expense both to his own peace of mind and—since people in misery usually make others feel miserable too—that of those around him.

'Plunge into the world!' Vivekananda therefore recommends, 'and then, after a time, when you have suffered and enjoyed all that is in it, will renunciation come; then will calmness come. So fulfil your desire for power and everything else, and after you have fulfilled the desire, will come the time when you will know that they are all very little things; but until you have fulfilled this desire, until you have passed through that activity, it is impossible for you to come to the state of calmness, serenity, and self-surrender'.

"I once met a man in my country whom I had known before as a very supid, dull person, who knew nothing and had not the desire to know anything, and was living the life of a brute.He asked me what he should do to know God, how he was to get free. 'Can you tell a lie?' I asked him. 'No', he replied. 'Then you must learn to do so. It is better to tell a lie than to be a brute, or a log of wood. You are inactive; you have not certainly reached the highest state, which is beyond all actions, calm and serene; you are too dull even to do something wicked'. That was an extreme case, of course, and I was joking with him; but what I meant was that a man must be active in order to pass through activity to perfect calmness''.

The path to salvation, then, is through the world; not by pretending that it does not exist.

Karma Yoga, if needs be, can dispense with Providence. Buddha achieved Nirvana (literally, 'waning away'—the waning away of desire and egocentricity), though he did not speak a word about 'grace' or God. He did, however, mention a higher existence that is changeless, deathless, and without limitation—the state of Buddhahood, where one has broken loose from the wheel of rebirth.

Can non-attachment co-exist with duty? What, specifically, is the Karma Yogi's conception of duty? Vivekananda believes that duty has no objective basis: 'It is not the thing done that defines a duty...Yet duty exists from the subjective side. Any action that makes us go Godward is a good action...; any action that makes us go downward is evil'.

'When an attachment has become established, we call it duty...It is, so to say, a sort of chronic disease...We baptise it with the high-sounding name of duty...There is no duty for you and me. Whatever you have to give to the world, do give by all means, but not as a duty...Be not compelled. Why should you be compelled? Everything that you do under compulsion goes to build up attachment'.

''A current rushing down of its own nature falls into a hollow and makes a whirlpool, and after running a little in that whirlpool, it emerges again in the form of the free current to go on unchecked. Each human life is like that current. It gets into the whirl, gets involved in the world of space, time, and causation, whirls round a little, crying out, 'My father! My brother! My fame!' and so on, and at last emerges out of it and regains its original freedom. The whole universe is doing that. Whether we know it or not...we are all working to get out of the dream of the world. Man's experience in the world is to enable him to get out of its whirlpool'.

Says Krishna, 'There is no rebirth once I am achieved', and in Revelation 3:12 of the Bible, we come across the following lines:

'Him that overcometh will I make a pillar in the temple of my God, and he shall go out no more'.

Can the theory of rebirth be verified?

To begin with, it is not the exclusive possession of Hindu philosophies, as is often assumed. For instance, Jesus, one has reason to believe, believed in it, though he was apparently skeptical of how the masses would take it. Talking of John the Baptist to the people who were expecting the Elias of former times to return, he said: 'And if ye will receive it, this is Elias, which was for to come'. (Matthew 11:14). And again: 'I say unto you, that Elias is come already, and they knew him not'. (Matthew 17:12).

Paul spoke of Esau and Jacob has having lived before.

As I have mentioned earlier, the tenet was not uncommon among the Greeks.

Buddha could supposedly recall his past lives.

The Mohammedan saint Maulavi Ram declared, 'Many lives and countless bodies we have seen'.

Kahlil Gibran's Prophet speaks thus: 'Yes, I shall return with the tide, and though death may hide me and the greater silence enfold me, yet again will I seek your understanding...Know, therefore, that from the greater silence I shall return...Forget not that I shall come back to you...A little while, a moment of rest upon the wind, and another woman shall bear me'.

Other believers in reincarnation include Geothe, John Donne, William Blake, and Salvador Dali.

'So what?' you might well retort. 'A number of wrongs do not make a right.'

Ever a votary of the truth, and nothing but the truth, Vivekananda qualifies his postulate: 'About the higher mysteries of life and existence I can do no more than speculate, as others do. Reincarnation seems to me to be the nearest to a logical explanation for many things with which we are confronted in the realm of religion. But I do not advance it as a doctrine. It is no more than a theory at best, and is not susceptible of proof except by personal experience, and that proof is good only for the man who has it. Your experience is nothing to me, nor mine to you'.

Nevertheless, he is quite convinced that the theory can stand its ground even under a close intellectual scrutiny: 'No other theory except that of reincarnation accounts for the wide divergence that we find between man and man in their powers to acquire knowledge.. First, let us consider the process by means of which knowledge is acquired. Suppose I go into the street and see a dog. How do I know it is a dog? I refer it to my mind, and in my mind are groups of all my past experiences, arranged and pigeon-holed, as it were. As soon as a new impression comes, I take it up and refer it to some of the old pigeon-holes, and as soon as I find a group of the same impression already existing, I place it in the group, and I am satisfied. I know it as a dog, becuase it coincides with the impressions already there. When I do not find the cognates of this new experience inside, I become dissatisfied. When, not finding the cognates of an impression, we become dissatisfied, this state of mind is called 'ignorance'; but, when finding the cognates of an impression already existing, we become satisfied, this is called 'knowledge'. When one apple fell, men became dissatisfied. Then gradually they found out the group. What was the group they found? That all apples fell, so they called it 'gravitation'. Now we see that without a fund of already existing experience, any new experience would be impossible, for there would be nothing to which to refer the new impression. So, if, as some of the European philosophers think, a child came into the world with what they call 'tabula rasa', such a child would never attain to any degree of intellectual power, because he would have nothing to which to refer his new experiences. We see that the power of acquiring knowledge varies in each individual; and this shows that each one of us has come with his own fund of knowledge. Knowledge can only be got in one way, the way of experience, there is no other way to know. If we have not experienced it in this life, we must have experienced it in other lives. How is it that the fear of death is everywhere? A little chicken is just out of an egg and an eagle comes, and the chicken flies in fear to its mother. There is an old explanation ( I should hardly dignify it by such a name). It is called instinct. What makes that little chicken just out of the egg afraid to die? How is it that as soon as a duckling hatched by a hen comes near water, it jumps into it and swims? It never swam before, nor saw anything swim. People call it instinct. It is a big word, but it leaves us where we were before. Let us study this phenomenon of instinct. A child begins to play on the piano. At first she must pay attention to every key she is fingering, and as she goes on and on for months and years, the playing becomes almost involuntary, instinctive. What was first done with conscious will does not require later an effort of the will'.

That's the first k. o. for disbelievers, and there's another coming: If instinct is independent of the will, then the will should have no control over it. 'Almost all the actions which are now instinctive can be brought under the control of the will. Each muscle of the body can be brought under control. This is perfectly well known... what we now call instinct is degeneration of voluntary actions; therefore, if the analogy applies to the whole of creation, if all nature is uniform, then what is instinct in lower animals, as well as in men, must be the degeneration of the will'.

If 'each involution presupposes an evolution, and each evolution an involution, we see that instinct is involved reason'.

Let us suppose—my apologies for taking this liberty— that, till last month, you were a 'chain smoker'. You lit a cigatette on waking up, on finishing a meal, on taking your seat in the bathroom, and on sundry other occasions. You could not think without the help of nicotine. But what with your propensity towards cancer, your doctor had firmly ruled out such indulgences. Fond as you are of being decently alive, one night you determinedly stubbed out the last cigarette of your last packet and broke into a contemptuous valediction. 'Get thee lost!' you said, maliciously eyeing the stumpy remnant of your cigarette. 'Thou hast turned into a scourge. I shall mooch thee no more'. And true to your purpose, you did not mooch it any more. At first it was agonising, but with every passing day your will slowly but surely asserted itself on what had once become an 'instinct'. Your will was no longer 'degenerate'.

Let's take another example. How often have we not just seen or met a person and formed an instant, 'instinctive' like or dislike for her or him. We make much of such phrases as 'the vibes are on' and 'he gives me bad vibes' and similar other expressions. A degree of familiarity sometimes arouses second thoughts about a person, and we say, 'He isn't what I thought he was', or 'I took him to be this or that, but it isn't true'. We may change our opinion and even grow to like a person we initially—and for no conscious reason—disliked, and vice versa. Anyone acquainted with the rudiments of psychology will be aware that such an occurrence may not be half as mysterious as it sounds. In fact, it may have a rationale of its own. Subconsciously, we have associated the person in question with behavioural patterns that can be traced back to someone we know or knew or heard about, with whom he has certain points of similarity—say, the cut of the face or the manner of speaking. But thanks to our changed attitude or the recognised arbitrariness of our logic, we manage to shed our predispositions and modify our views. In other words, what we first mistook for 'instinct' was no more than 'involved reasons'—a reason which, when we found it unsound, we were able to conquer by a natural exercise of our will.

When Vivekananda uses the word 'degeneration' with reference to the will, he uses it functionally and not with any moral overtones. He would be the last person to denounce such indispensable 'instincts' as the instincts for self-preservation or knowledge.

"The latest scientific men are coming back to the ancient sages", Vivekananda says, "and as far as they have done so, there is perfect agreement. They admit that each man and each animal is born with a fund of experience, and that all these actions in the mind are the result of past experience. 'But what', they ask, 'is the use of saying that that experience belongs to the soul? Why not say it belongs to the body, and to the body alone? Why not say it is hereditary transmission?...Why not say that all the experience with which I am born is the resultant effect of all the past experience of my ancestors? The sum total of the experience from the little protoplasm up to the highest human being is in me, but it has come from body to body in the course of hereditary transmission. Where will the difficulty be?'

"This question is very nice, and we admit some part of this hereditary transmission. How far? As far as furnishing the material. We, by our past actions, conform ourselves to a certain birth in a certain body, and the only suitable material for that body comes from the parents who have made themselves fit to have that soul as their offspring".

"The simple hereditary theory takes for granted the most astonishing proposition without any proof, that mental experience can be recorded in matter, that mental experience can be involved in matter ('matter' here, one presumes, refers to 'gross' matter and not to the mind. The degree of grossness is an important determinant of receptivity in matter. Thus a blow with the fist will leave no mark on a rock, but will make a deep impression on a mass of dough). When I look at you, in the lake of my mnid there is a wave. That wave subsides, but it remains in fine form, as an impression. We understand a physical impression remaining in the body. But what proof is there that the mental impression can remain in the body...? Even granting it were possible for each mental impression to remain in the body, that every impression, beginning from the first man down to my father, was in my father's body, how could it be transmitted to me? Through the bioplasmic cell? How could that be?...The same parents may have a number of children; then, from this theory of hereditary transmission, where the impression and the impressed (that is to say, material) are one, it rigorously follows that by the birth of every child the parents must lose a part of their own impressions, or, if the parents should transmit the whole of their impressions, then, after the birth of the first child, their minds would be a vacuum. (This is a curious mistake. As far back as 1858 the German pathologist Rudolf Virchow had concluded that the cell reproduces itself by nuclear division).

"Again, if in the dioplasmic cell the infinite amount of impressions from all time has entered, where and how is it?"

The Karmic theory dispenses with the possibility of any chance or accidental element in human life and emphasizes the essentially causal character of all existence. (No soul bears the burden of another, as the Koran says). It teaches personal responsibility and asserts that nobody can get anything unless he earns it. Oddly enough, many Westerners see it as an odious Oriental absurdity sowing the seeds of fatalism and submissive indolence. The misconception is not difficult to fathom, for it probably originated in India itself. Put yourself in the garb of an oppressive member of the Indian ruling classes. A walking corpse of a peasant comes to you, fearfully voicing a few grievances. In his precarious struggle for sheer survival he has somehow saved up some wee left-overs of daring. How do you tackle the situation? What do you say? It's simple. Pat comes your answer: 'Your're poor, ill-clothed, half-starved, miserable? Very well! You must have been a pretty depraved lot in your previous lives — so what the hell are you grumbling about? You want to skip your penalties? In other words, you want to challenge God's law? No? Then get along and be satisfied. Come, come be a man! Wipe your tears. Good boy'. Tyranny by divine sanction!

It has been urged that the notion of retribution and reward does not quite fit in with the idea of a benevolent and omnipotent Brahman, for is it not true that He Himself is helpless against its workings? But this is like asking whether God could make a square circle. Aquinas very aptly observed that such questions were foolish, since God could not be self-contradictory. If He created a world which moved on certain immutable laws, He would contradict Himself by destroying its regularity. Imagine the sun rising in the west one day!

But God is all-merciful all the same. Says Vivekananda, 'Our religion does not take away from mankind the mercy of the Lord. That is always there. He stands beside this tremendous current of good and evil. He the bondless, the ever-merciful, is always ready to help us to the other shore, for His mercy is great, and it always comes to the pure in heart'.

Is not Jesus a personification of God's mercy? For he, the sinless, suffered the most racking pains to redeem mankind:

And he went forward a little, and fell on the ground, and prayed that, if it were possible, the hour might pass from him.

And he said, Abba, Father, all things are possible unto thee; take away this cup (of suffering) from me: nevertheless not what I will, but what thou wilt'.

Krishna assures Arjuna that every time the forces of vice become over-powering in the world, he will incarnate as man. This, the Vedantists maintain, is God's mercy at work; for by descending into this phenomenal existence, he paves the way for the rest. 'God understands human failings and becomes man to do good to humanity', says Vivekananda. He suffers with mankind and then blazes the trail to emancipation. He does not stand aloof and give pompous speeches. Instead, he exposes himself to the same miseries—if not greater, as in Jesus's case—that human beings are heir to, and by transcending them, gives a living example of how others too may do so.

More on this later.

John the Revelator says in Revelations 3:12 that he was told in a vision that whoever should overcome the material world would no longer have to go out from the kingdom of heaven. This could not be more in consonance with the law of Karma, according to which, as we have noted, the soul is kept in the thraldom of matter until the mind is overcome. In some persons it is a thin, delicate film that veils the soul. These persons are close to enlightenment. In others the covering is a thick, opaque sheath; their proprietors have a good deal of scraping and washing to do before they can get a glimpse of the holy city.

'According to the Vedantists, when this body dissolves, the vital forces of the man go back to his mind and the mind becomes dissolved, as it were, into the Prana, and that Prana enters into the soul of man, and the soul of man comes out, clothed, as it were, with what they call the fine body, the mental body or spiritual body, as you may like to call it. In this body are the Samskaras of the man. What are the Samskaras? The mind is like a lake, and every thought is like a wave upon the lake. Just as in the lake waves rise and then fall down and disappear, so these thought-waves are continually rising in the mind-stuff and then disappearing, but they do not disappear for ever. They become finer and finer, but they are all there, ready to start up at another time when called upon to do so. Memory is simple calling back into wave-form some of those thoughts which have gone into that finer state of existence. Thus, everything that we have thought, every action that we have done, is lodged in the mind; it is all there in fine form, and when a man dies, the sum total of these impressions is in the mind, which again works upon a little fine material as a medium. The soul, clothed, as it were, with these impressions and the fine body, passes out, and the destiny of the soul is guided by the resultant of all the different forces represented by the different impressions. According to us, there are three different goals for the soul.

'Those that are very spiritual, when they die, follow the solar rays and reach what is called the solar sphere, through which they reach what is called the lunar sphere, and through that they reach what is called the sphere of lightning, and there they meet with another soul who is already blessed, and he guides the new-comer forward to

the highest of all spheres, which is called the Brahmaloka,
the sphere is Brahma, There these souls attain to
omniscience and omnipotence, become almost as powerful and all-knowing as God Himself; and they...become
one with the Universal at the end of the cycle. The next
class of persons, who have been doing good work with
selfish motives, are carried by the results of their good
works, when they die, to what is called the lunar sphere,
where there are various heavens; and there they acquire
fine bodies, the bodies of gods. They become gods and live
there and enjoy the blessing of heaven for a long period;
and after that period is finished the old Karma is again
upon them, and so they fall back again to the earth...The
last class, namely, the wicked, when they die, become
ghosts or demons, and live somewhere midway between
the lunar sphere and this earth. Some try to disturb mankind, some are friendly; and after living there for sometime they also fall back to the earth and become animals.
After living for some time in a animal body they get
released, and come back, and become men again, and thus
get one chance to work out their salvation. We see, then,
that those who have nearly attained to perfection, in
whom only very little of impurity remains, go to the
Brahmaloka through the rays of the sun; those who were a
middling sort of people, who did some good work here
with the idea of going to heaven, go to the heavens in the
lunar sphere and there obtain god-bodies; but they have
again to become men and so have one more chance to
become perfect. Those that are very wicked become
ghosts and demons, and then they may have to become
animals; after that they become men again and get another
chance to perfect themselves. This earth is called the
Karma-Bhumi, the sphere of Karma. Here alone man
makes his good or bad Karma. When a man wants to go to
heaven and does good works for that purpose, he becomes a
god and does not as such store up any bad Karma. He just
enjoys the effects of the good work he did on earth; and
when his good Karma is exhausted, there comes upon him
the resultant force of all the evil Karma he had previously

stored up in life, and that brings him down again to this earth. In the same way, those that become ghosts remain in that state, not giving rise to fresh Karma, but suffer the evil results of their past misdeeds, and later on remain for a time in an animal body without causing any fresh Karma. When that period is finished, they too become men again. The states of reward and punishment due to good and bad Karmas are devoid of the force of generating fresh Karmas; they have only to be enjoyed or suffered. If there is an extraordinarily good or an extraordinarily evil Karma, it bears fruit very quickly. For instance, if a man has been doing many evil things all his life, but does one good act, the result of that good act will immediately appear, but when the result has been gone through, all the evil acts must produce their results also. All men who do certain good and great acts, but the general tenor of whose lives has not been correct, will become gods; and after living for some time in god-bodies, enjoying the powers of gods, they will have again to become men; when the power of the good acts is thus finished, the old evil comes up to be worked out. Those who do extraordinarily evil acts have to put on ghost and devil bodies, and when the effect of those evil actions is exhausted, the little good action which remains associated with them, makes them again become men...

'Man, therefore...is the greatest being that is in the universe, and this world of work the best place in it, because only herein is the greatest and the best chance for him to become perfect. Angels or gods, whatever you may call them, have all to become men...This is the great centre, the wonderful poise, and the wonderful opportunity—this human life'.

Now who's going to buy this, and for how much? It sounds so thoroughly eccentric and freaky!—like the idea of television did a century back, I remember mentioning to an unlettered lady, quite a few years ago, that man had reached the moon. She was a lady of high spirits, and thumped me on the back, and began to roll with laughter. I tried desperately to explain to her that it wasn't a joke, at which she got serious and chided me for trying to pull her leg. I got her (literate) son to confirm the fact, but to no avail. For how on earth, or, to put it more literally, how on moon could such a thing be?

One of the functions of education, as I see it, is to teach people to suspend their judgement until the matter in question can be objectively examined. If this is not possible, the only reasonable course for them to adopt would be one of open-minded neutrality. It is doubtful how many of us will have occasion to probe into the mysteries of after-death phenomena, but that gives us no leave to condemn the conclusions of those who have done so. Science, after all, is still a baby, a bit precocious may be, and rather proud, but with miles to go and lots to see. Sometimes it will revel in playing the 'big daddy', but don't you take it too seriously; it's just growing!

Be that as it may, the above theory of the soul's destiny has some significant and fascinating implications:

Man is the prize of creation because, in all creation, he alone possesses free will. There ARE such things as gods and goddesses and angels and fairies (remember Joan of Arc?) and evil spirits, which are not discernible to the common eye.* (Incidentally, Yogis believe in a usually dormant non-physical third eye at the centre of the forehead which, if opened through yogic practices, confers supernatural sight). Nevertheless, though these ethereal beings might possess powers that are, in some ways, superior to man's it is man alone who enjoys the opportunity to make of himself what he will(s). He is the master of his own destiny, and his destiny is the outcome of his Karma. (Which is why the Buddhists say, 'Karma is my own; I am the inheritor of my Karma; Karma is my creator, Karma is my friend and refuge. I shall reap the consequences of whatever Karma I do, good or bad'.)

From the perspective of all his lives on earth as a human being, man possesses complete free will; but in so far as,

* Of the numerous first-hand accounts of such phenomena, one of special interest to this writer was the late ex-Viceroy of India Lord Dufferin's recollection of his encounter with a 'ghost'—a spectre which, for some unacountable reason, chose to save his life.

through these various lives, he has already created a stock of Karma, his destiny is naturally not independent of them.

The full ethical impact of the doctrine of reincarnation is perhaps nowhere more tellingly stated as in the following quote from the present Dalai Lama's 'My Land and My People'.

'Belief in rebirth should engender a universal love because all living beings and creatures, in the course of their numberless lives and our own, have been our beloved parents, children, brothers, sisters, friends. And the virtues our creed encourages are those which arise from this universal love: tolerance, forbearance, charity, kindness, compassion'.

Empirically, the question of rebirth is still a very intriguing one. Parapsychologists, in trying to unravel its tangles, have inevitably had to cut their way through numerous cases of fraud. Regrettable as these hoaxes are and much as they have done to cater to the appetite of cynics, they do not, obviously, refute the theory itself.

Dr H.N. Banerjee, as Research Director of the Indian Institute of Parapsychology, Benaras, looked into 750 instances of alleged rebirth around the world. He took care to adopt stringent measures to ascertain the bona-fides of his subjects and came across a good many apparently authentic cases of children with what he calls 'Extra Cerebral Memory'. Among these was the case of a nine-year-old Punjabi girl named Mohini, who claimed to have lived in New York a century ago. On being flown to New York, the girl readily identified 'her' house and evinced a startlingly accurate knowledge of the persons who had once resided there.

However, such testimonies, though encouraging, are not fool-proof.

To date, the enigma of child prodigies remains unsolved. Neither heredity nor the sub-conscious (if it is a product of the present life) explains it. Seemingly there are only two logical possibilities: Jung's collective (or inherited) unconscious—which leaves a few stones unturned—and the law of Karma which, in effect, is vastly dissimilar to Jung's hypothesis, there being no room in it for unaccounted and unmerited windfalls.

Vivekananda feels that 'such a gigantic will as that of a Buddha or a Jesus could not be obtained in one life, for we know who their fathers were. It is not known that their fathers ever spoke a word for the good of mankind. Millions and millions of carpenters like Joseph had gone; millions are still living. Millions and millions of petty kings like Buddha's father had been in the world. If it was only a case of hereditary transmission, how do you account for this petty prince who was not, perhaps, obeyed by his own servants, producing this son whom half a world worships? How do you explain the gulf between the carpenter and his son whom millions of human beings worship as God?... The gigantic will which Buddha and Jesus threw over the world, whence did it come? Whence came this accumulation of power? It must have been there through ages and ages, continually growing bigger and bigger, until it burst on society in a Buddha or a Jesus...'

'The whole of this life which slowly manifests itself from the protoplasm to the perfected human being—the Incarnation of God on earth*—the whole of this series, is but one life, and the whole of this manifestation must have been involved in that very protoplasm. This whole life, this very God on earth, was involved in it and slowly came out, manifesting itself slowly, slowly, slowly...Take off all ideas of growth from your mind. With the idea of growth is associated something coming from outside, something extraneous, which would give the lie to the truth that the Infinite which lies latent in every life is independent of all external conditions. It can never grow; it was always there, and only manifests Itself'.

Subjectively, perfection lies beyond goodness. Goodness and evil are, after all, twin brothers, and both are bastards of the mind. When, in your school days, you fell into a spelling error, your teacher may have made you sit down and copy out the word correctly five or ten times in succession, till at last it got hammered into your head. The next day your teacher, deciding to test you, asked you the spelling again, and you thought back and brought it out slowly but correctly. It was a conscious process. You

---

* There would seem to be an ambivalence in Vivekananda's attitude towards Incarnations: on the one hand they have evolved themselves into perfection, and on the other they are perfection become, as it were, 'finitised' for divine ends. The first viewpoint would certainly seem more reasonable. See also 'The Religion of Love'.

were right, but it was a determined effort. As the days progessed and you used the word more and more often you gradually established your mastery over it, and suddenly you didn't have to think back for it any more. You could spell it out like that, unhesitatingly, automatically. It didn't involve any thought, you didn't tell yourself, 'Yes, this time I've got it!', because subconsciously you were aware that you couldn't possibly do otherwise.

Similarly, the student of spirituality thinks deliberate good thoughts and performs deliberate acts of purity to frustrate the inroads of corruption and depravity. Next, he has to rise above this consciousness of correctness, for the truly spiritual person is nobody's slave—not even his virtue's! When he reaches this level he is said to be 'inspired'—he can do whatever he wishes without breaking the moral law.

Ramakrishna used to say that when a thorn got stuck in your flesh, you picked up another thorn to remove the first, and when that was done, you threw both away. In the same manner, you have to remove bad acts with good ones, and then dispense with both.

Have you ever considered yourself generous? Yes? Then here's a mighty blow for you:

'When you give something to a man and expect nothing...his ingratitude will not tell upon you, because you never expected anything, never thought you had any right to anything in the way of a return. You gave him what he deserved; his own Karma got it for him; your Karma made you the carrier thereof. Why should you be proud of having given away something? You are the porter that carried the...gift, and the world deserved it by its own Karma. Where is then the reason for pride in you?'

Spirituality is not like football or mathematics or astronomy. You don't 'do' it at a certain time and not do it at another. You have always to carry it with you—yes, even into the bedroom and the bathroom! It's the substructure on which you have to build each and every moment of your life:

'It is a hard fight and a weary one, this
   fight of the truth-seeker; for the
   vow of the truth-seeker is more

hard than that of the warrior, or
of the widowed wife who would
follow her husband.
For the warrior fights for a few hours
and the widow's struggle with
death is soon ended:

But the truth-seeker's battle goes on
day and night, as long as life lasts
it never ceases'.

Kabir

# Raja Yoga: The Royal Road *

MANY, MANY DAYS have passed. All these days Guru Nanak, the founder of the Sikh religion, has had no food. Is he weak, hungry, miserable? No, he still looks fresh. He is alive and kicking. What does he live on?

He lives on air. That's right—air!

Albecerius. Carthaginian medium and diviner. St. Augustine's student is sceptical and wants to test him. He asks, 'What am I thinking about now?' Albecerius has hardly had an education, but he promptly quotes a passage from Virgil. 'That's what you are thinking about', he says. The student is dazzled. He acquiesces.

Times have changed, and now it is 1974. Uri Geller, former nightclub magician from Israel, is presently in California, bending a fork he does not touch. He just sits and concentrates on it!

The Menninger Foundation in Topeka, Kansas, finds that subjects can learn to lower their hand temperature 10° by 'willing' the movement of a temperature meter connected to the skin. There are others who can stop their own migraines by monitoring the blood flow to their faces and so reducing arterial swelling.

Vivekananda hears and smiles. He smiles at our scepticism or our open-mouthed bewilderment. Hasn't he seen enough of such things? Hasn't he, er, indulged a bit in them himself?—And when certain creeps in America sought his acquaintance with ulterior motives, didn't he give them the shivers by reading their minds?

How are such things done?

'According to the Raja-Yogi, the external world is but the gross form of the internal, or subtle. The finer is always the cause, the grosser the effect. So the external world is the effect, the internal the cause. In the same way external forces are simply the grosser parts, of which the internal forces are the finer. The man who has discovered and learned how to manipulate the internal forces will get the whole of nature under his control. The Yogi proposes to

---

* Strictly speaking, Raja Yoga is not within Vedanta, though Vivekananda, generally known as a Vedantist, incorporated it into his philosophy.

himself no less a task than to master the whole universe, to control the whole of nature. He wants to arrive at the point where what we call 'nature's laws' will have no influence over him, where he will be able to get beyond them all. He will be master of the whole of nature, internal and external'.

Now think: what is the nature of cause and effect? You paint a picture. What causes it?—The thought behind it. Could you have painted otherwise? You hit someone. First you are angry, first the thought of anger arises in you, and then you follow it through, you hit. Who said it was bad to build castles in the air? You can't have them on the ground unless you first build them in the air! That's the law: the subtle first and then the gross, the unseen first and then the seen. God's will was the cause of the universe, and the universe itself was the effect of that will.

'Gather a shell from the strewn beach
    And listen at its lips; they sigh
The same desire and mystery
    The echo of the whole sea's speech.
And all mankind is thus at heart
    Not anything but what thou art:
And Earth, Sea, Man, are all in each'.

The microcosm reflects the macrocosm. Both are built on the same plan, both have the same origin. Thought created all. Control thought and you control everything. There is nothing mysterious or occult about that. Its as obvious as the skin on your face.

'We...know that the greatest power is lodged in the fine, not in the coarse. We see a man take up a huge weight, we see his muscles swell, and all over his body we see signs of exertion, and we think the muscles are powerful things. But it is the thin thread-like things, the nerves, which bring power to the muscles; the moment one of these threads is cut off from reaching the muscles, they are not able to work at all. These tiny nerves bring the power from some-thing still finer, and that again in its turn brings it from something finer still—thought, and so on. So, it is the fine that is really the seat of power. Of course we can see the movements in the gross; but when fine movements take place, we cannot see them...But if by any science, any investigation, we are helped to get hold of these finer forces which are the cause of the expression, the expre-. ssion itself will be under control. There is a little bubble coming from the bottom of a lake; we do not see it coming all the time, we see it only when it bursts on the surface; so, we can perceive thought only after they develop a great deal, or after they become actions...If we can get control over the fine movements, if we can get hold of thought at the root, before it has become thought, before it has become action, then it would be possible for us to control the whole. Now, if there is a method by which we can analyze, investigate, understand, and finally grapple with those finer powers, the finer causes, then alone is it possible to have control over ourselves, and the man who has control over his own mind assuredly will have control over every other mind. That is why purity and morality have been always the object of religion; a pure, moral man has control of himself'.

When Jesus healed, they called it a miracle. What is a miracle? A supernatural event, says the dictionary. 'Applied Raja Yoga', says the Yogi. Just because you don't understand it, you call it a miracle. We know what its about. Its natural to us. Did not Jesus tell his disciples that they too could learn to do the same? How? Through Raja Yoga. Call it that or call it what you will, so long as it means the same.

'Since the dawn of history', says Vivekananda, 'various extraordinary phenomena have been recorded as happening amongst human beings. Witnesses are not wanting in modern times to attest to the fact of such events, even in societies living under the full blaze of modern science. The vast mass of such evidence is unreliable, as coming from ignorant, superstitious or fraudulent persons. In many instances the so-called miracles are imitations. But what do they imitate? It is not the sign of a candid and scientific mind to throw overboard anything without proper investigation. Surface scientists, unable to explain the various extraordinary mental phenomena, strive to ignore their very existence. They are, therefore, more culpable than those who think that their prayers are answered by a being, or beings, above the clouds, or than those who believe that their petitions will make such being change the course of the universe'.

Jung's eminent student Hans Jacobs says: 'That many yogins, outstripping all accomplishments feasible under hypnosis, can bring breathing and heartbeats to a standstill for many hours and that some, who have specialized in this, are even able to swallow concentrated nitric acid or cyanide of potassium without adverse effects, or to produce fire by rubbing their arms, or can make themselves invisible even to the photographic plate—such facts, though not unknown to individual scientists, have been more or less ignored by official science'.

'For thousands of years', continues Vivekananda, 'such phenomena have been studied, investigated, and generalised, the whole ground of the religious faculties of man has been analyzed, and the practical result is the science of Raja-Yoga. Raja-Yoga does not, after the unpardonable manner of some modern scientists, deny the existence of facts which are difficult to explain; on the other hand, it gently, yet in no uncertain terms, tells the superstitious that miracles and answers to prayers, and powers of faith though true as facts, are not rendered comprehensible through the superstitious explanation of attributing them to the agency of a being, or beings, above the clouds. It declares that each man is only a conduit for the infinite ocean of knowledge and power that lies behind mankind. It teaches that desires and wants are in man, that the power of supply is also in man; and that wherever and whenever a desire, a want, a prayer has been fulfilled it was out of this infinite magazine that the supply came, and not from any supernatural being. The idea of supernatural beings may rouse to a certain extent the power of action in man, but it also brings spiritual decay. It brings dependence; it brings fear; it brings superstition. It degenerates into a horrible belief in the natural weakness of man. There is no supernatural, says the Yogi, but there are in nature gross manifestations and subtle manifestations. The subtle are the causes, the gross the effects. The gross can be easily perceived by the senses; not so the subtle. The pratice of Raja-Yoga will lead to the acquisition of the more subtle perceptions'.

Used properly, cocaine kills pain. Used wrongly, it ravages man. Used properly, Raja Yoga evolves Supermen; used wrongly, lunatics. Time and again men have been knocked off their senses fumbling through its difficult exercises. It brooks no indiscipline, it tolerates no fancy whims. First get a good master, it says, before you dare touch me: I've grown tired of filling asylums!

It will be discreet to skip the details of this Yoga par excellence. 'Lead us not into temptation, but deliver us from evil, Amen'. Raja Yoga, or literally, the Royal Yoga, is not for everyone, as Vivekananda is careful to stress. More importantly, 'with few exceptions', as he adds. 'Yoga (Raja Yoga is often simply termed 'Yoga') can only be safely learned by direct contact with a teacher'.

As for the numerous powers the Yogi is supposed to acquire 'the knowledge of past and future', the capacity to read another's mind*, to become invisible, to walk on water, to understand all animal sounds, to gain supernatural touch, tastes, etc. —we are told that 'these are, as it were, to be met in the way; and if the Yogi rejects them, he attains the highest. If he is tempted to acquire these, his further progress is barred'. 'We must not stop by the way or allow ourselves to be dazzled by these beads of glass when the mine of diamonds lies before us'. The 'beads of glass' will, nevertheless, serve to verify the practicality of the Yogic exercises and inspire us to keep working at them.

---

*HORIZON, WINTER 1974, Vol. XVI, No. 1 THE COSMOS IS A GAINT THOUGHT by Robert Hughes: 'To know what others are thinking is one of the basic dreams (and episodic nightmares) of man, and thought is his last privacy. When one finds the Russian and American governments tacitly involved in ESP research, one may be reasonably sure that the object of interest is strategic and has to do with power'.

The temptations of Christ and Buddha, allegorically represented through the Devil and the demon Mara respectively, would seem to have cropped up at this phase of their Yoga. 'The human mind, however, is so weak', observes Vivekananda, 'that, not to speak of householders, even ninety per cent of the Sadhus happen to be votaries of these powers'.

These are the 'false prophets' who, in the words of Jesus, may 'come to you in sheep's clothing, but inwardly they are ravenous wolves. Ye shall know them by their fruits. Do men gather grapes of thorns, or figs of thistles?'

'It's a plausible guess', said the Oxford philosopher H.H. Price, 'that many of our everyday thoughts and emotions are telepathic or partly telepathic in origin'.

Vivekananda had expressed the same view three-quarters of a century earlier. Just as light-waves from the distant stars travel for years before they reach our planet, he asked, could not thought-waves travel the atmosphere till a properly-tuned human antenna could pick them up? There are men 'who really know the power of thought; they are sure that, even if they go into a cave and close the door and simply think five true thoughts and then pass away, these five thoughts of theirs will live through eternity. Indeed such thoughts will penetrate through the mountains, cross the oceans, and travel through the world. They will enter deep into human hearts and brains and raise up men and women who will give them practical expression in the working of human life...Many of the greatest men in the world have passed away unknown'.

Elucidating on the function of Raja Yoga, Vivekananda says: 'Deep down in our subconscious mind are stored up all the thoughts and acts of the past...This great, boundless ocean of subjective mind is full of all the thoughts and actions of the past. Each one of these is striving to be recognised, pushing outward for expression, surging, wave after wave, out upon the objective mind, the conscious mind. These thoughts, this stored-up energy, we take for natural desires, talents, etc. It is because we do not realise their true origin. We obey them blindly, unquestioningly, and slavery, the most helpless kind of slavery, is the result, and we call ourselves free. Free!

'The ghosts of past thoughts...hold us down. All the misery of the world is caused by this slavery to the senses. Our inability to rise above the sense-life—the striving for physical pleasures—is the cause of all the horrors and miseries in the world.

'It is the science of psychology that teaches us to hold in check the wild gyrations of the mind, place it under the control of the will, and thus free ourselves from its tyrannous mandate. Psychology is therefore the science of sciences without which all sciences and all other knowledge are worthless.

'The mind uncontrolled and unguided will drag us down, down forever, rend us, kill us; and the mind controlled and guided will save us, free us. So it must be controlled, and psychology will teach us how to do it.

'Deep, deep within, is the soul, the essential man, the Atman, Turn the mind inward and become united to that, and from that standpoint of stability, the gyrations of the mind can be watched and facts observed...Such facts, such data, are to be found by those who go deep enough, and only by such.

'If you intend to study the mind, you must have systematic training; you must practise to bring the mind under your control, to attain to that consciousness from which you will be able to study the mind and remain unmoved by its wild gyrations'.

That is precisely what Yoga sets out to do.

The famous American psychologist and philosopher William James, who was wont to record the personal testimonies of those who had experienced mental renewal, makes the following observations on Yoga:

'But the most venerable ascetic system, and the one whose results have the most voluminous experimental (?) corroboration is undoubtedly the Yoga system in Hindustan...The result claimed, and certainly in many cases accorded by impartial judges, is strength of character, personal power, unshakability of soul...A very gifted European friend of mind...by persistently carrying out for several months its method of fasting from food and sleep, its exercises in breathing and thought-concentration, and its fantastic posture-gymnastics, seems to have succeeded in waking up deeper levels of will and moral and intellectual power in himself, and to have escaped from a decidedly menacing brain-condition of the 'circular' type, from which he had suffered for years...A profound modification has unquestionably occurred in the running of his mental machinery. The gearing has changed, and his will is available otherwise than it was'.

And all this only in the preliminary stages of Yoga, for Yoga takes years to master, and sometimes a life-time is hardly enough!

We shall now move on to the 'Eightfold Path' of Yogic discipline:

YAMA: abstention. It comprises of the 'thou shalt nots' of Yoga. The novice is to refrain from injury in thought, word, or deed; from falsehood, covetousness, passions and lust, and from acceptance of gifts, 'even when' says Vivekananda, 'one is suffering terribly...The idea is, when a man receives a gift from another...he loses his independence, he becomes bound and attached'.

NIYAMA: regular habits and observances—austerity, study, contentment, internal and external purity, fasting or in other ways controlling the body, and devotion to God (this, though beneficial, is considered optional. The Yogi maintains that the student can reach God eventually, in any case).

As for internal purity, Vivekananda would perhaps like to recite the following lines!

Then let your secret thoughts be fair—
They have a vital part, and share
In shaping words and moulding fate;
God's system is so intricate.

External purity includes cleanliness concerning clothes and diet. The Yogi is warned to avoid extremes. Self-mortification is emphatically ruled out. Austerity is simplicity rather than self-torture. At one stage Buddha, on being too severe with himself, gained nothing thereby and, on the contrary, almost lost his life. He came to the conclusion that asceticism, taken beyond certain bounds, leads one to desire the very objects one is trying to renounce. Thus, prolonged and habitual denial of food will give one, if anything, a voracious appetite.

The path to follow, then, is the golden mean.

'Repeating the Vedas and other Mantras, by which the Sattva material in the body is purified, is called study', says Vivekananda.

The reading of scriptures is purifying because it is auto-suggestive. Purification of the mind automatically leads to purification of the body.

The next item is the repetition of Mantras. Perhaps no portion of the Hindu religion has been more widely misunderstood. A Mantra is summarily dismissed as a 'formula of worship' or a 'prayer' or as 'mystic syllables', with no attempt to comprehend its purport. In point of fact, however, it goes much deeper, and involves the metaphysics of sound. This is an extremely complex subject, and an exposition of its subtleties could easily fill a tome. However, we shall touch on the topic very lightly and, like Vivekananda, concern ourselves here primarily with the generic Mantra 'Om'.

'What's in a name?' asked Shakespeare, to which Vivekananda would wink and reply, 'There's more to it, William, than is dreamt of in your philosophy.'

'In the beginning was the Word', says the Bible, 'and the Word was with God and the Word was God'. Much in the same vein the Vedas declare: 'In the beginning was Brahman with whom was Vak (or 'the Word'), and the Vak is Brahman'.

According to the scriptures, sound precedes creation. Sound is the cause, and not the effect of vibration. 'Sound creates air, atmosphere, and climate, and then only it reaches the stage of vibration. When it reaches the stage of vibration, sound creates light. Light is nothing but sound of a particular frequency...Every object is the result of a particular density of sound. That is its seminal sound'.*

* Justice P. B. Mukharji, Intr., 'Japasutram' by Swami Pratyagatma-nanda Saraswati, Ganesh and Co., Madras.

A small experiment in physics provides a hint as to how sound produces light. 'If a glass rod is made to vibrate vigorously at ultrasonic frequencies and is then held between the finger and the thumb, it burns the skin. The reason is that sound is producing fire and light.

'By the silent sound of high frequency, one can, by the gentlest touch of the softest material, cut through the hardest rock or glass...If water is vibrated in ultrasonic frequencies, it can kill aquatic creatures'.

The power of sound in creating mental states and their physical counterparts is perhaps nowhere more obvious than in music. Music can soothe your mind and relax your body, arouse your feelings and activate your muscles, and indeed beget each and every mood that the emotions are capable of. Try to think without sound—that is, in this case, without words, and see if you can ever succeed. The two are as much a part and parcel of each other as a book and its pages. Every mental picture we visualize has a silent or spoken word behind it.

Phenomenal existence is an existence in names and forms. Everything with form has a corresponding 'natural name'. This is 'the sound inherent in every object of the world. Every object has in it a system of constituting forces, which are in ceaseless movement and produce sound. But this sound is of the supersonic order, not audible to the normal ear of common men; partially audible to the yogic ear and...fully audible to the Absolute Ear...Once J. C. Bose performed an experiment to demonstrate the existence of inaudible sound—inaudible to the ordinary human ear but audible to an ear manufactured by him, which, he said, was powerful enough to pick up any sound, however high or low, like the ear of a Yogi of yore'.§

The natural name of an object is called its 'Bija-Mantra' or 'Seed-Mantra'. As picked up by the Yogic ear, the

¶Justice P. B. Mukharji, Intr., 'Japasutram' by Swami Pratyagatmananda Saraswati, Ganesh and Co., Madras.
§Charu Chandra Chatterji, Intr., 'Japasutram' by Swami Pratyagatmananda Saraswati.

primordial sound, the seminal sound of all names and all
forms is Om (pronounced 'Aum'). This is the sound constantly emanating from the kinetic, phenomenal aspect of
Brahman. In the transcendental quiescent Brahman there
is neither name nor sound, the two, as we have seen, being
inextricably linked with each other. Sound precedes this
universe of name and form, and Brahman, needless to say,
precedes sound.

'All things are created by the Om', sings Kabir. 'The
love-form is His body'. And again:

> Receive that Word from which the
>     Universe springeth!
> That Word is the Guru: I have heard
>     it, and become the disciple.
> How many are there who know the
>     meaning of that Word!
> O Sadhu, practise that Word!
> The Vedas and the Puranas proclaim it,
> The world is established in it,
> The Rishis and devotees speak of it:
> But none knows the mystery of the word.
> The householder leaves his house when
>     he hears it,
> The ascetic comes back to love when
>     he hears it,
> The Six Philosophies* expound it,
> The Spirit of Renunciation points to
>     that Word,
> From that Word the world-form has
>     sprung,
> That Word reveals all.
> Kabir says: 'But who knows whence
>     the Word cometh?'

---

*A reference to the 6 philosophical systems that had sprung up within
Hinduism and which, though sometimes differing widely, were all
considered 'orthodox' by virtue of being inspired by the Vedas.

Conceived of as such, the Mantra is none other than Ishwara Itself, that is, Brahman in Its mobile, Maya-ic aspect—in Its aspect of ruler of the phenomenal universe.

'In the universe', says Vivekananda, 'Brahman...or the Cosmic first manifested himself as name, and then as form, i.e. as this universe. All this expressed sensible universe is the form behind which stands...the manifester as Logos or Word'. The manifester is the Logos. 'The Word was with God and the Word was God' —and the Word IS God, and the Word is 'Om'.

'Om (Aum) is...the basis of all sounds', Vivekananda explains. 'The first letter, A, is the root sound, the key, pronounced without touching any part of the tongue or palate. M represents the last sound in the series, being produced by the closed lips, and the U rolls from the very root to the end of the sounding board of the mouth. Thus Om represents the whole phenomena of sound-production'. It is 'the natural symbol, the matrix of all the various sounds. It denotes the whole range and possibility of all the words that can be made.'

Yogic discipline recommends repetition of 'Om' and meditation on its meaning. The method is not only auto-suggestive, but has an intrinsic value on the strength of its acoustic properties. It is the 'Sabda—Brahman' or the 'Word—God'. It spiritualizes the system and eventually reveals the immanent Brahman.

All other Mantras, then, are necessarily derivatives of this Master Mantra. Vivekananda does not go into them. However, it may be mentioned in passing that pronunciation, volume, and proper intonation play an indispensable role in making a Mantra effective. To be efficacious it must be practised under the guidance of a suitable Guru. One has to carry on till the power of the Mantra has made a sufficient impress in our inner beings so that the hidden Divinity may reveal Itself. Swami Ramdas, who left us not so long ago, achieved the state of superconsciousness through the repetition of God's name alone. He says, 'People say that we must first concentrate the mind upon some object; after concentration is fully achieved we should start meditation upon the qualities or attributes of the Divine within. Then we get lost in Him and we rise above body-idea. We then experience a state of trance or Samadhi. No such process was gone through by Ramdas. Repetition of God's name was the only Sadhana he did for the first two years... Chanting the Name for two years produced a state of superconciousness in which the body was forgotten', 'You are really repeating the name of your own immortal Self' etc. However, he lays down a few essential prerequisites for success—renunciation, a keen longing for God, and a 'meaningful' repetition of the Mantra, that is, establishing a spiritual identity with the Name, and not merely chanting it by rote.

Tne Guru, who is required to have developed the Yogic ear, discovers the acoustic equivalent of the immanent Brahman in a particular individual, and initiates that person accordingly. A Mantra, because a good deal of its power lies in its intrinsic qualities, ceases to be such in translation.

Says Ramakrishna: 'Knowingly or unknowingly, consciously or unconsciously, in whatever state we utter His name, we acquire the merit of such utterance. A man who voluntarily goes into a river and bathes therein gets the benefit of the bath; so does likewise he who has been pushed into the river by another, or who while sleeping soundly has water thrown upon him by another'.

We shall now take up the next 'limb' of Yoga:

ASANA: Posture, or steady and comfortable posture. While practising Yoga, 'a series of exercises, physical and mental, is to be gone through every day, until certain higher states are reached. Therefore it is quite necessary that we should find a posture in which we can remain long. That posture which is the easiest for one should be the one chosen. For thinking, a certain posture may be very easy for one man, while to another it may be very difficult. We will find later on that...a good deal of activity goes on in the body. Nerve currents will have to be displaced and given a new channel. New sorts of vibrations will begin, the whole constitution will be remodelled, as it were. But the main part of the activity will lie along the spinal column, so that the one thing necessary for the posture is to hold the spinal column, free, sitting erect, holding the three parts—the chest, neck, and head—in a straight line. Let the whole weight of the body be supported by the ribs, and then you have an easy natural posture, with the spine straight'.

PRANAYAMA: 'Prana means the vital forces in one's own body; Ayama means controlling them'. Loosely, Pranayama is referred to as breath-control, and consists of three parts: inhalation, retention, and exhalation. The time relation between these three phases of respiration is extremely important, but varies according to different traditions. Vivekananda recommends the ratio of 1:2:1. 'This breathing must be done with rhythmic regularity'. It purifies the system, is beneficial to health, and an aid to concentration. Breathing is 'the fly-wheel of the whole bodily system.

It acts first upon the lungs, the lungs act on the heart, the heart acts upon the circulation, this in turn upon the brain, and the brain upon the mind. The will can produce an outside sensation, and the outside sensation can arouse the will'.

Pranayama can have adverse effects if it is not performed under expert supervision.

It is interesting to note that the Indian mystic philosopher Aurobindo assigns a particularly high value to Pranayama. 'It is my experience', he says, 'that Pranayama makes one's intellect sharper and one's brain quicker. When I was doing it in Baroda, I was practising it for about five or six hours per day, three hours in the morning and two or three hours in the evening. I felt that there was a great accession of light and power in the mind. I used to write poetry in those days. Earlier, I could sometimes write only about two hundred lines a month. After I began practising Pranayama, I could write two hundred lines in half an hour. My memory was rather dull before. But afterwards, I composed whenever I had inspiration, and remembered ad seriatum the whole, till I committed it to paper at leisure. I felt as if my brain was encircled by a ring of electricity'.

PRATYAHARA: Sense-withdrawal—the stepping-stone to concentration. The Yogi tries to hold in check all the affective reactions to the stimuli of the external world. 'The organs of the senses are acting outwards and coming in contact with external objects. Bringing them under the control of the will is what is called Pratyahara or gathering towards oneself...He who has succeeded in attaching or detaching his mind to or from the centres at will has succeeded in Pratyahara...When we can do this, we shall really possess character...A man, to prove that he is not a machine, must demonstrate that he is under the control of nothing...It is tremendous work...only after a patient, continuous struggle for years can one succeed'.

How is it practised? Aldous Huxley, in his essay on the 'Technique of Timeless Realization', gives an eloquent exposition on this aspect of the liberatory method. 'Man triumphs over his imaginative automatisms', he says, 'not by pitting himself against them, but by CONSCIOUSLY allowing them free play; his attitude towards them is one of active neutrality...Man rules by dividing; refusing to take sides with any of his mental forces, he permits them to neutralize one another'.

Says Vivekananda: 'The mind ranges over wide circles of thought and those circles widen out into ever increasing circles, as in a pond when we throw a stone into it. We want to reverse the process and starting with a huge circle make it narrower until at last we can fix the mind on one point and make it stay there'.

DHARANA: 'Holding the mind to one point'. Pratyahara evolves into Dharana, as it were, which in turn evolves into Dhyana. 'It is possible to acquire miraculous powers by attaining even a little degree of mental concentration', notes Vivekananda.

DHYANA: Yogic meditation, as distinct from meditation as it is generally understood, where it means 'to revolve in the mind'. Here there is no 'revolving', but one-pointed concentration. If asked how, in that case, Dhyana is any different from Pratyahara, the Yogi replies that the former comprises a markedly greater intensity of concentration than the latter. In Dhyana the Yogi can, as it were, pass beyond the outer coverings, the mere appearance of the object he is concentrating on, and preceive the inner nature of its being, 'the subtle infra-atomic constituents', as Kovoor T. Behanan puts it, 'which make up the ultimate elements of matter'.

What object should the Yogi choose to concentrate on? Usually a favourite image of a divinity is recommended. Vivekananda, however, tackles the subject in the light of his own meditative practices:

'First, the practice of meditation has to proceed with some one object before the mind. Once I used to concentrate my mind on some black point. Ultimately...I could not see the point any more, nor notice that the point was before me at all—the mind used to be no more—no wave of functioning would rise, as if it were all an ocean without any breath of air. In that state I used to get glimpses of supersensuous truth. So I think the practice of meditation even with some trifling external object leads to mental concentration. But it is true that the mind very easily attains calmness when one practises meditation with anything on which one's mind is most apt to settle down. This is the reason why we have in this country so much worship of the images of gods and goddesses...The fact...is that the objects of meditation can never be the same in the case of all men...The real aim is to make the mind functionless'.

A story tells of a king who was obsessed with jewellery, of which he owned aplenty. One day a Yogi held forth to him on the emptiness of worldly possessions, and tried to impress upon him the futility of setting such great store by his wealth. Only the path of religion could lead to real happiness, he said.

The king, having given the Yogi an attentive ear, observed that, what with all his royal responsibilities, he could not possibly become an ascetic, and he therefore asked the Yogi to suggest some method whereby he could follow the religious path without having to renounce the world.

Knowing full well the king's weakness for jewellery, the Yogi asked the king to concentrate on the diamond of his bracelet. Eager to learn, the king did so without much difficulty, for he felt a natural affinity towards the object of his concentration. And as he continued the practice, his mind attained purity.

A disciple of Swamiji queries: But if the mind becomes completely engrossed and identified with some object, how can it give us the consciousness of Brahman?'

Vivekananda replies: 'Though the mind at first assumes the form of the object, yet later on the consciousness of that object vanishes. Then only the experience of pure "isness" remains', the experience of Samadhi.

SAMADHI: Literally, concentration. Actually, the summit of concentration, where the subject merges into the object: the knower and the known become one. "All the different steps in Yoga are intended to bring us scientifically to the super-conscious state, or Samadhi...This meditative state is the highest state of existence. So long as there is desire no real happiness can come. It is only the contemplative, witness-like study of objects that brings to us real enjoyment and happiness...To him who desires nothing, and does not mix himself up with them, the manifold changes of nature are one panorama of beauty and sublimity...Then will all sorrows cease, all miseries vanish...and the soul will be free for ever'.

A saying attributed to Jesus in a Coptic manuscript, 'The Gospel According To Thomas', goes:

When you make the two one, and
when you make the inner as the outer
and the outer as the inner and the above
as the below...
then you shall enter (The Kingdom)...
I am the Light that is above
them all, I am the All,
the All came forth from Me and the All
attained to Me. Cleave a (piece of) wood, I
am there; lift up the stone and you will
find Me there'.

This, in fact, is what Samadhi is about. If we take the analogy of a lake whose surface has been lashed into waves, the bottom of the lake which is then hidden from view is the Soul or the Atman. The waves themselves are the mind. When the waves of the mind have been stilled, the calm surface (the still mind) reveals the Soul—the ultimate Reality, the Abode of Everlasting Bliss. In that state there is no time, space, or causation for as Vivekananda observes, 'Time begins with mind, space also is in the mind...Without the idea of succession there cannot be any idea of causation. Time, space and causation, therefore, are in the mind'.

In Samadhi or trance-contemplation, all sense of body-consciousness is lost. The universe is seen not as a dis-jointed cluster of separate units but as a harmonious whole. And man has finally succeeded in—to use Vivekananda's term—'de-hypnotising' himself from all illusions of his own littleness, and realizing himself as a self-sufficient totality.

The fault, dear Brutus, is not in our stars, but in ourselves, that we are underlings!

Samadhi, by whatever name it may go, whether is it the Nirvana of Buddha or the Satori of Zen Buddhists, or the Hindu Moksha or Mukti or the entrance to the Christian 'Kingdom of Heaven', is an ineffable experience. Words only exist in this phenomenal existence, this universe of form. The transcendental state is, by definition, beyond speech—which is why the supremely practical Buddha, when asked to describe its nature, replied by keeping the silence. 'Do not dip the string of thought into the unfathomable', he said later; 'he who questions errs, he who answers errs'; but many have, nevertheless, ambi-tiously gone ahead and attempted to do just that. Among them is Vivekananda. Here I reproduce a portion of his poem, 'The Song of the Free', where he recollects the beatitude of the Supreme Moment:

Nor angel I, nor man nor brute,
Nor body, mind, nor he nor she;

The books do stop in wonder mute
To tell my nature—I am He!

Before the sun, the moon, the earth,
Before the stars or comets free,
Before e'en Time has had its birth
I was, I am, and I will be!

The beauteous earth, the glorious sun,
The calm sweet moon, the spangled sky,
Causation's laws do make them run,
They live in bonds, in bonds they die—

And mind its mantle, dreamy net
Casts o'er them all and holds them fast,
In warp and woof of thought are set
Earth, hells or heavens, or worst or best.

Know these are but the outer crust—
All space and time, all effect, cause,
I am beyond all sense, all thought,
The Witness of the Universe!

Not two nor many, 'tis but One.
And thus in me all ones I have
I cannot hate, I cannot shun
Myself from me—I can but love!

From dreams awake, from bonds be free!
Be not afraid. This mystery,
My shadow, cannot frighten me!
Know once for all that I am He!

# The Religion of Love

WHAT, IS THE nature of love? You love your baby, you say. How do you give it expression? By wanting to be with it, to play with it, by sharing its joy when it bubbles with mirth, by sensing its discomforts and tending to its needs, by keeping it away from harm, etc.—isn't it? These are some of the expressions of your love. What is the one common characteristic of all these acts? What is the one common motive force behind them all? The feeling of being one with, and inseparable from, the baby, isn't it? When your baby falls sick, you do not curse it. You do not say, 'To hell with it! Now I've got to waste money on a doctor!' However short of money you may be, you somehow try to see to it that your baby gets all the treatment it needs. Why is it so?—Because when your baby is not well, neither are you well, for the child is you and you are the child. That is love. Do you expect anything in return for your love? Return from whom? From yourself? If a car comes dashing towards your baby do you step aside to save your own life? Would you not rather save your baby's, even if it has to be at the cost of your own?

Says Vivekananda: 'We may represent love as a triangle, each of the angles of which corresponds to one of its inseparable characteristics. There can be no triangle without all its three angles; and there can be no true love without its three following characteristics. The first angle of our triangle of love is that love knows no bargaining. Wherever there is any seeking for something in return, there can be no real love; it becomes a mere matter of shopkeeping. As long as there is in us any idea of deriving this or that favour from God in return for our respect and allegiance to Him, so long there can be no true love growing in our hearts. Those who worship God because they wish Him to bestow favours on them, are sure not to worship Him if those favours are not forthcoming. The Bhakta loves the Lord because He is lovable; there is no other motive originating or directing this divine emotion of the true devotee'.

As a good example of this one may cite the following outpouring of the French mystic, Francois de Sales:

'While, O God, I see your sweet face, and know that the song of my love pleases You, alas, what comfort I find!... But when You turn away Your eyes, and I no longer see in Your sweet favour that You were taking pleasure in my song, O true God, how my soul suffers! But I do not stop loving You...or singing the hymn of my love, not for the pleasure I find in it, for I have none, but for the pure love of Your pleasure'.

Vivekananda continues: 'The second angle of the triangle of love is that love knows no fear...It is a degradation to worship God through fear of punishment...So long as there is any fear in the heart, how can there be love also? Love conquers naturally all fear'.

Vivekananda could well have extended the connotation of the word 'fear', for surely love knows no fear in more senses than one: if it is true that you cannot love a person you fear, it is equally true that you are able to summon the will to face a potential or actual threat to your loved one, however much this may endanger your own person. Your love will endure through fortitude, scandal, and resistance, and you will woo the worst danger for the weal or safety of your beloved.

'The third angle of the triangle is that love knows no rival, for in it is always embodied the lover's highest ideal. True love never comes until the object of our love becomes to us our highest ideal...What is it that the world commonly worships?...That ideal which men and women commonly worship is what is in themselves; every person projects his or her own ideal on the outside world and kneels before it'.

As first sight, the third angle might seem slightly amiss. True, you love your ideal, but do you love only your ideal? Is it a universal principle?—Do you necessarily love your child because it is the ideal, or do you rather love it just because it is your child? What if it is dull and ugly? Will you then not love it because it does not embody your ideal of intelligence and beauty?

Vivekananda would say that this is confused question-ing. Let us assume that your child is dull and ugly. These, of course, are not your ideals, and yet you love it. What do you love in it? Not its dullness, surely, nor, obviously, its ugliness. What does this imply? It implies that when love is true, its object is the very act of loving. That itself is its ideal. In loving we free ourselves of psychological prison-walls, we extend ourselves. Love sings, because it is the most joyful, fulfilling experience in life, and its song is always of light and freedom and expansion, never of gloom and confinement. As Thoreau said, 'Birds never sing in caves'.

Love brings out your best, makes you a better human being—which is another way of saying it makes you a better you. And because you can only become a better you by following your own path, by climbing up your own spiritual ladder rather than somebody else's, by a process of self-discovery rather than by conformity with any external standards, true love brings you closer to yourself.

To love is to live, and therefore the true lover's ideal is loving itself. The true lover loves the growth, the vitality and the sense of sharing that love brings, and in the very act of loving he is amply recompensed.

Yet another thing—what made you have a child? Was it just the sexual act? What made you want to be a mother or a father? Have you analyzed it?—It is your unconscious craving for permanence, for immortality! It is your unconscious craving for God! Deep down in you, whether you know it or not, you want to last for ever and ever. You are innately infinite, may be you do not know it, but the infinite in you is asserting itself in infinite ways'.

Bhakti is spiritual love—spiritual love directed towards God. Vivekananda quotes from "the king of Bhaktas, Prahlada: 'That deathless love which the ignorant have for the fleeting objects of the senses—as I keep meditating on Thee—may not that intense love for Thee slip away from my heart!" Love for whom? For the Supreme Lord... Love for any other being, however great, cannot be Bhakti; for, as Ramanuja says...'all things that live in the world are slaves of birth and death caused by karma; therefore they cannot be helpful as objects of meditation, because they are all in ignorance and subject to change.'''

Bhakti-Yoga, or the religion of love, is not everyone's cup of tea. It is only for those who are primarily emotional and have religious faith.

What is religious faith? Is it a crutch for those who are feeble and unsure of themselves? Is it a vice-parading -as-virtue of cowards and hypocrites? Is it mere superstition? Religious faith apart, what indeed is faith?

Faith comes in two varieties—it can be provisional or concrete.

Provisional faith is a hypothetical trust on something or someone which or who you have reason to believe has a fair possibility of delivering the goods that you seek. It is precisely this faith which, shall we say, makes you buy a book which you are perfectly aware might eventually disappoint you, but which, by fliping through its pages, you feel will be good. It is this same faith that may make you vote for a political party that may or may not stand by its election promises. This faith is essentially a matter of calculated conjecture, and is behind every invention and a good many discoveries.

The well-known astronomer Sir Edward Appleton says: '...I want to make the assumption which the astronomer—and indeed any scientist—makes about the universe he investigates. It is this: that the same physical causes give rise to the same physical results anywhere in the universe, and at any time, past, present, and future...The scientist... makes the assumption...as an act of faith; and he feels confirmed in that faith by his increasing ability to build up a consistent and satisfying picture of the universe and its behaviour'.

The process is in no way dissimilar to that used in the three Yogas that we have considered so far, but in Bhakti Yoga the neophyte begins not with an assumption, but with an intuitive certainty of spiritual reality. Though people tend to frown on such words as 'intuition', it is a faculty that is exploited by the scientist. In 'The Faith of the Physicist', Dr H.H. Huntley writes that he 'is driven by his own experience to conclude that his personality has depths and resources beyond the analysing conscious mind wherein lie...a latent skill and wisdom superior to that to which his consciousness is routinely accustomed'.

This is 'concrete' faith where reason actually plays a secondary role.

Blind faith is also 'concrete', but it is irrational. It is not that reason plays a scondary role here—it does not play a role at all. Faith here does not transcend reason, but fails to reach up to it. Vivekananda is aware of the fact that Bhakti Yoga is particularly susceptible to such faith. 'Its great disadvantage', he says, 'is that in its lower forms it oftentimes degenerates into hideous fanaticism. The fanatical crew in Hinduism, or Mohammedanism, or Christianity, have always been almost exclusively recruited from these worshippers on the lower planes of Bhakti. That singleness of attachment to a loved object, without which no genuine love can grow, is very often also the cause of the denunciation of everything else. All the weak and undeveloped minds in every religion or country have only one way of loving their own ideal, i.e. by hating every other ideal...This kind of love is somewhat like the canine instinct of guarding the master's property from intrusion; only, the instinct of the dog is better than the reason of man, for the dog never mistakes its master for an enemy in whatever dress he may come before it'.

Concrete religious faith, if it is not to be blind and therefore harmful, must be rooted in personal spiritual experience. It might be wondered if this would not limit Bhakti only to the saints and prophets, who constitute but a minute percentage of mankind and are perhaps now, more than ever, a fast diminishing breed. But it is not unlikely that the mystic element in our iives is more common than is generally admitted, or even realized. Sometimes it is clear-cut enough to be its own verification. At other moments it appears only to flit by swiftly, leaving us a trifle bewildered but not without a lingering aroma of its heady perfume. Such, however, are the prejudices of our times that we tend to feel a bit ashamed of acknow-ledging these experiences, and dismiss them as inconse-quential abberations into irrationality. And thus an occurence that might well have been an introductory gateway to a new and better vision of life is soon lost in the pits of oblivion.

Scientists themselves could not be more alive to the mysteries of life. After all, were it not so, science would soon come to a standstill. It was Einstein, I think, who walked up to Yehudi Menuhin after a performance by the latter and said something to the effect of, 'Now that I've heard you play, I'm convinced that God exists'.

Mystic perceptions are intuitive. While intuitions, loosely speaking, might be right or wrong, they are, in a stricter sence, well-based apprehensions. So-called 'flashes of inspiration' can, of course, be peculiar devia-tions of the mind resulting from some sort of hypnotic suggestion (drugs and music, for example, may sometimes create delusions which seem very real while they last), but that by no means precludes the fact that there is a definite intuitive faculty in man. Perhaps the most widely accepted exemplars of this are the poets and the artists.

All Yogas are in essence nothing but a means to develop this inspirational aptitude latent in man, so that it can be brought to the surface and drawn from at will. Thus, what is normally purely involuntary and occurs by fits and starts, if at all, becomes, for the Yoga adept, both a voluntary and a sustained act.

Bhakti involves unconditional belief in a Surprene Being. This faith is necessarily built on a neurotic fantasy unless the person in question has been fortunate enough to have had an intuitive revelation. Thus Einstein's state-ment, 'My religion consists of a humble admiration of the illimitable Superior Spirit who reveals Himself in the slight details we are able to perceive with our frail and feeble mind. That deeply emotional conviction of the presence of a superior Reasoning Power which is revealed in the incomprehensible universe, forms my idea of God', is typically a scientist's expression of Bhakti.

Revelations, of course, can take any number of forms; and however much others may try to persuade him that his experience must have been hallucinatory, it usually impinges on the recipient's mind with all the inexorable force of a strong internal mandate:

St. Paul, in a poem by F.W.H. Myers, says,

'Whoso has felt the spirit of the Highest
Cannot confound nor doubt Him nor deny;
Yea with one voice, O world, though thou deniest,
Stand thou on that side, for on this am I'.

It may be instructive to point out the 'tests' by which such 'mandates' may be supposed to be authentic, for so-called revelations may, after all, be delusive.

To use the words of Christ, 'By their fruits ye shall know them'. In the religiously inspired person, says Vivekananda, the 'love of the pleasures of the senses and of the intellect is all made dim and thrown aside and cast into the shade by the love of God Himself'. 'Of all renunciations, the most natural, so to say, is that of the Bhakti-Yogi. Here, there is no violence, nothing to give up, nothing to tear off, as it were, from ourselves, nothing from which we have violently to separate ourselves; the Bhakta's renunciation is easy, smooth-flowing, and as natural as the things around us. We see the manifestation of this sort of renunciation, although more or less in the form of caricatures, every day around us. A man begins to love a woman; after a while he loves another, and the first woman he lets go. She drops out of his mind smoothly, gently, without his feeling the want of her at all...A man loves his own city, then he begins to love his country; and the intense love for his little city drops off smoothly, naturally. Again, a man learns to love the whole world; his love for his country, his intense, fanatical patriotism drops off without hurting him, without any manifestation of violence. An uncultured man loves the pleasures of the senses intensely; as he becomes cultured, he begins to love intellectual pleasures, and his sense-enjoyments become less and less. No man can enjoy a meal with the same gusto or pleasure as a dog or a wolf; but those pleasures which a man gets from intellectual experiences and achievements, the dog can never enjoy...In human society, the nearer the man is to the animal, the stronger is his pleasure in the sense; and the higher and the more cultured the man is, the greater is his pleasure in intellectual and such other finer pursuits. So, when a man gets even higher than the plane of the intellect, higher than that of mere thought, when he gets to the plane of spirituality and of divine inspiration, he finds there a state of bliss, compared with which all the pleasures of the senses, or even of the intellect, are as nothing. When the moon shines brightly, all the stars become dim; and when the sun shines, the moon herself becomes dim. The renunciation necessary for the attainment of Bhakti is not obtained by killing anything, but just comes in as naturally as in the presence of an increasingly stronger light, the less intense ones become dimmer and dimmer until they vanish away completely'.

The noephyte Bhakti Yogi is one who has had involuntary flashes of mystical insight and bliss and seeks to prolong and ultimately perpetuate those fleeting moments of beatitude.

Here are two of the many well-known and documented accounts of mystical experiences which, I hope, will throw light on the makings and the nature of the Bhakti temperament. The passages are from Penguin Books' 'Mysticism: A Study And An Anthology', by F.C. Happold.

'It happened in my room in Peterhouse in the evening of 1 February 1913, when I was an undergraduate at Cambridge. If I say that Christ came to me I should be using conventional words which would carry no precise meaning; for Christ comes to men and women in different ways. When I tried to record the experience at the time I used the imagery of the vision of the Holy Grail; it seemed to me to be like that. There was, however, no sensible vision. There was just the room, with its shabby furniture and the fire burning in the grate and the red-shaded lamp on the table. But the room was filled by a Presence, which in a strange way was both about me and within me, like light or warmth. I was overwhelmingly possessed by Someone who was not myself, and yet I felt I was more myself than I had ever been before. I was filled with an intense happiness, an almost unbearable joy, such as I had never known before and have never known since. And over all was a deep sense of peace and security and certainty.

Though I now recognize the experience as of the kind described by the mystics, at that time I knew nothing of mysticism'.

Of the talented girl Simone Weil 'with her philosophical genius and rare powers of thought', F.C. Happold writes that her spiritual autobiography 'Waiting on God' is 'of peculiar interest for our times. In it she tells how, as an adolescent, though remaining within the Christian inspiration, she saw the problem of God as one insoluble for the human mind. So she decided to leave it alone, neither affirming nor denying anything. Prayer she avoided since she feared its power of suggestion; she desired above all to keep her intellectual integrity'.

At the age of twenty-nine 'she spent ten days from Palm Sunday to Easter Tuesday at Solesmes, following, in spite of the splitting headaches to which she was subject, all the liturgical services. There she met an English Catholic, who introduced her to the English metaphysical poets of the seventeenth century. Thus she came in contact with George Herbert's poem 'Love', which she learnt by heart and used to recite to herself'.

Now Simone Weil herself takes over:

'It was during one of these recitations that...Christ himself came down and took possession of me.

'In my arguments about the insolubility of the problem of God I had never foreseen the possibility of that, of a real contact, person to person, here below, between a human being and God. I had vaguely heard of things of this kind, but I had never believed in them. In the Fioretti the accounts of apparitions rather put me off if anything, like the miracles in the Gospels. Moreover, in this sudden possession of me by Christ, neither my senses nor my imagination had any part; I only felt in the midst of my suffering the presence of a love, like that which one can read in the smile of a beloved face...God in his mercy had prevented me from reading the mystics, so that it should be evident to me that I had not invented this absolutely unexpected contact.

'Yet I still half refused, not my love but my intelligence. For it seemed to me certain, and I still think so today, that one cannot wrestle enough with God if one does it out of pure regard for truth'.

Wordsworth's 'Excursion' provides a good example of the realisation of God as an Impersonal Being:

'He beheld the sun
Rise up, and bathe the world in light! He looked—
Ocean and earth, the solid frame of earth
And Ocean's liquid mass, in gladness lay
Beneath him—Far and wide the clouds were touched,
And in their silent faces could be read
Unutterable love. Sound needed none,
Nor any voice of joy; his spirit drank
The spectacle; sensation, soul and form,
All melted into him; they swallowed up
His animal being; in them did he live,
And by them did he live; they were his life.
In such access of mind, in such high hour
Of visitation of the living God,
Thought was not; in enjoyment it expired.
No thanks he breathed, he proferred no request,
Wrapt into still communion that transcends
The imperfect offices of prayer and praise,
His mind was a thanksgiving to the Power
That made him; it was blessedness and love'.

Did not Christ tell us, 'Ye have not chosen me but I have chosen you'?

Though Vivekananda often repeats that Bhakti is the easiest of the Yogas, it can only be so because, I maintain, the Bhakta starts from a spiritual vantage-point. You cannot love a hypothetical Being; neither, even were you certain that It existed, would you necessarily have loved It. Love implies direct communication, and the Bhakta must have had it—else his belief is a hoax.

Ramakrishna saw and loved God as Rama and Siva and Kali and Krishna and Jesus and others. He says, 'As the same fish is dressed into soup, curry, or cutlet, and each has his own choice dish in it, so the Lord of the Universe, though one, manifests Himself differently according to the different likings of His worshippers'. 'The God with form is visible, nay, we can touch Him face to face, as with one's dearest friend'. 'God is formless, and is with form too, and He is that which transcends both form and formlessness. He alone can say what else He is'. 'As water when congealed becomes ice, so the visible form of the Almighty is the materialised manifestation of the allpervading formless Brahman...As the ice, being part and parcel of the water, remains in the water for a time and afterwards melts in it, so the Personal God is part and parcel of the Impersonal. He rises from the Impersonal, remains there, and ultimately merges into it and disappears'.

We have already considered the necessities of anthropomorphism in a previous chapter. 'Bhakti, then, can be directed towards Brahman only in His personal aspect', says Vivekananda. 'The way is more difficult for those whose mind is attached to the Absolute. Bhakti has to float on smoothly with the current of our nature'.

'True it is that we cannot have any idea of Brahman which is not anthropomorphic, but is it not equally true of everything we know?...Therefore to say that Ishwara (i.e. Brahman in His relative conditioned aspect) is unreal, because He is anthropomorphic, is sheer nonsense...The idea of Ishwara covers all the ground ever denoted and connoted by the word real, and Ishwara is as real as anything else in the universe'. '...human consciousness is one of the elements in the make-up of all the objects of our perception and conception, internal as well as external. Beginning with our bodies and going up to Ishwara, we may see that every object of our perception is this consciousness plus something else, whatever that may be; and this unavoidable mixture is what we ordinarily think of as reality. Indeed it is, and ever will be, all the reality that is possible for the human mind to know'

In other words, Ishwara or the personal God is the highest possible representation of the Absolute in the relative universe. Avataras or Incarnations of God are all manifestations of Ishwara. Says Krishna:

'When goodness grows weak,
When evil increases,
I make myself a body.
In every age I come back
To deliver the holy,
To destroy the sin of the sinner,
To establish righteousness'.

Vivekananda would contest the claim that Jesus was the 'only begotten son of God' and would look at it, perhaps, as an ignorant and unwarranted superimposition by his disciples.

The term 'Incarnation' might seem paradoxical. Does not any human being who attains transcendental consciousness, and can maintain it at will, become 'God incarnate'? Do not, for instance, the highest saints qualify for this title?

No, says Bhakti Yoga. 'For one thing, the Incarnation's birth is not the outcome of past Karma, as it is with the saints; it is a result of free choice. And for another, the Incarnations' powers are far superior to the saints'. Thus Krishna gave divine sights to Arjuna by a mere wish. 'Be clean' Jesus said to a leper, and at once the leprosy left the man. A touch from Ramakrishna could make men illumined. Says Vivekananda's Guru: 'When a huge tidal wave comes, all the little brooks and ditches become full to the brim without any effort or consciousness on their own part; so when an Incarnation comes, a tidalwave of spirituality breaks upon the world, and people feel spirituality almost full in the air.'

It may be objected that the basis of the distinctions between an Incarnation and a saint are somewhat arbitrary and inconsistent. After all, if the saint has reached pure consciousness, does it not automatically follow that he acquires all the spiritual boons that are naturally conjoined to it?

Here again it would be best to begin by quoting Ramakrishna: 'A liberated man overcomes the world of Karma, and though he continues to live and work, he is not bound or tainted by it. He lives only to exhaust what are known as the Prarabdha Karmas.' (Prarabdha Karmas are the stored-up Karmas of the past which are yet to be resolved in the present life). This would imply that while an Incarnation is born and lives beyond Karma, the saint wins enlightenment even prior to his perfection. As soon as he overcomes the law of cause and effect, he dies in the body and melts into the Absolute.

This might trigger another difficulty: does it mean that a person may be, at one and the same time, both enlightened and imperfect?

Yes, he may. In fact, he cannot be both perfect and alive in the temporal world. While the Incarnation, the personified will of God, may even suffer on that account, the man who has gained Mukti or salvation has only done so by God's grace. In so far as he can never again do any wrong, and automatically does only the right things, he is, in a sense, perfect; but in so far as he has past Karmas to work off, he remains imperfect.

Ramakrishna says that 'the breeze of God's grace is always blowing; set your sails to catch this breeze'. God is full of mercy and prefers to season justice with mercy.

Does that make God contradictory? Let's try to see the point through a convenient comparison: Your little son has broken his sister's toy. The punishment normally meted out to him for committing such offences is to deprive him of his favourite sweet-dish. On this occasion, however, he has not only apologised to his sister, but has replaced her toy with one of his own. His penance earns him his sweet-dish, but you do not replace his toy till his next birthday. Thus he gets both justice and mercy.

(All said and done, let me let you in here on a little personal secret: this theory of Incarnations leaves me quite amused. Vivekananda holds Ramakrishna to be an Incarnation, but if, as Ramakrishna says, 'when an Incarnation comes, a tidal wave of spirituality breaks upon the world, and people feel spirituality almost full in the air', then isn't it odd that while, roughly a hundred years after Jesus—whom both Ramakrishna and Vivekananda consider an Incarnation—not more than five out of a hundred people believed in his Messiahship, in a similar time-span after Karl Marx's death, close to one-third of the human population is under the direct influence of Marxist ideas? And it is not inconceivable that Ramakrishna's own ideas have fewer genuine adherents in his own country than those of Vatsyayana, the celebrated third century A.D. author of the classic treatise on sex, the Kama Sutra.)

Vivekananda reminds us that Buddha had said that he would appear again after five hundred years, and after five hundred years appeared Christ. Wonder of wonders! But the greater wonder is that Buddha himself asserted that everyone has in him/her the potential to attain Buddhahood.

So where does that leave us?—

1. Perhaps both you and I are potential Avataras. Amen! Since our limitations stand in the way of our grasping the divine essence, we do so through people who realised their potential to various levels far higher than ours and thus, in the eyes of society, came to be recognised as Messiahs and Messengers.

2. However high the level of our spiritual evolution, the fact remains that we are imperfect beings not incapable of error. And therefore, as Ramakrishna will remark again a few pages later, 'Take the pearl

and throw the oyster-shell away'—or, to put it
bluntly, take the good and leave the bad.)

The Bhakti Yogi is initially asked to worship God
through any Incarnation or Personal God of his choice.
Says Vivekananda: 'By our present constitution we are
limited and bound to see God as man. If, for instance, the
buffaloes want to worship God they will, in keeping with
their own nature, see Him as a huge buffalo; if a fish wants
to worship God, it will have to form an idea of Him as a big
fish; and man has to think of Him as man'.

'Two kinds of men do not worship God as man—the
human brute who has no religion, and the Paramahamsa
(saint) who has risen beyond all the weaknesses of
humanity and has transcended the limits of his own
nature. To him all nature has become his own self. He
alone can worship God as He is'.

From the particular you proceed to the general. From
the unit you proceed to the many, and then the whole. As a
word is built up from individual letters, a sentence from
words, and a paragraph from sentences, so in love you
progress by including more and more. You cannot love the
Cosmic Impersonal without first loving the God Incarnate; you cannot love the God Incarnate without first
loving mankind; you cannot love mankind without first
loving your neighbour; and you cannot love your neighbour without first loving yourself (which is why the
Christian Gospel says, 'Love thy neighbour as thyself').

Loving yourself does not mean becoming a boast, for
boasting is more often than not a defence-mechanism
against intrusive feelings of inferiority. Loving yourself
implies, rather, having qualities in yourself that, in your
own eyes, makes you worthy of love. Loving yourself
implies having certain standards of your own and living
upto them. You cannot love yourself if you have sold your
soul to society, if you are always marching to somebody
else's drum-beats. Loving yourself means exploring your
own individuality and living creatively—and it is only by
such living that you can appreciate individuality in another
and come closer to loving him.

How often we slap a label on a person—'Communist', 'Capitalist', 'Christian', 'Hindu', 'Negro'—and, by so doing, refuse to acknowledge him as a separate human being. The fact, however, is that no two capitalists or Christians or Hindus or whatever—right down to two twins and two person's fingerprints—were ever exactly alike or will ever be so. As long as we fail to realise this, how is it possible for us to love one another?

Bhakti starts only after you have climbed the first rungs of the spiritual ladder.

There is an interesting anecdote about the Hindu saint Chaitanya who, it may be said, was the very embodiment of the religion of love. In his youth he immersed himself in serious study. His teacher was the renowned Vasudeva, who was also the teacher of another brilliant pupil called Raghunath, with whom he later established the Neo-logic of the Bengal school.

It is said that Raghunath was at work on what was later to become his famous treatise on logic, when he happened to hear that Chaitanya was writing a book on a similar topic. The two being friends, the former asked the latter if he would read out a few of his passages. However, when Chaitanya did so, his friend turned glum. 'What's wrong?' Chaitanya asked. Raghunath replied: 'I cherished a hope of leaving a name behind me, but I realize that my work will not be read if yours is shown to the public'. 'That's a small matter', said Chaitanya, 'don't you bother about it!' And so saying, he flung his manuscript into the Ganges.

Jesus at the Sermon on the Mount was superlative on the prerequistes of Bhakti: 'If thou art offering thy gift at the altar, and there rememberest that thy brother has anything against thee, leave thy gift before the altar and go first to be reconciled to thy brother, and then come and offer thy gift'. 'To him who asks of thee, give; and from him who would borrow of thee, dont turn away'. "You have heard that it was said, 'Thou shalt love thy neighbour, and shall hate thy enemy'. But I say to you, love your enemies, do good to those who hate you, and pray for those who persecute and calumniate you, so that you may be children of your Father in heaven, who makes his sun to rise on the good and the evil, and sends rain on the just and the unjust''.

The neophyte Bhakta begins his worship anthropo-morphically and ritually. 'Bhakti...is divided into the pre-paratory and the supreme forms...In the preparatory stage we unavoidably stand in need of concrete help to enable us to get on; and indeed the mythological and symbolic parts of all religions are natural growths which early environ the aspiring soul and help it Godward. It is also a significant fact that spiritual giants have been produced only in those systems of religion where there is an exuberant growth of rich mythology and ritualism. The dry fanatical forms of religion which attempt to eradicate all that is poetical, all that is beautiful and sublime, all that gives a firm grasp to the infant mind tottering in its Godward way—the forms which attempt to break down the very ridge-poles of the spiritual roof, and in their ignorant and superstitious con-ceptions of truth try to drive away all that is life-giving, all that furnishes the formative material to the spiritual plant growing in the human soul—such forms of religion too soon find that all that is left to them is but an empty shell, a contentless frame of words and sophistry, with perhaps a little flavour of a kind of social scavengering or the so-called spirit of reform'.

Nevertheless, 'Bhakti-Yoga lays on us the imperative command not to hate or deny any one of the various paths that lead to salvation. Yet the growing plant must be hedged around to protect it until it has grown into a tree. The tender plant of spirituality will die if exposed too early to the action of a constant change of ideas and ideals. Many people, in the name of what may be called religious liberalism, may be seen feeding their idle curiosity with a continuous succession of different ideals. With them, hearing new things grows into a kind of disease, a sort of religious drinkmania. They want to hear new things just by way of getting a temporary nervous excitement, and when one such exciting influence has had its effect on them, they are ready for another. Religion is with these people a sort of intellectual opium-eating, and there it ends'

'There is another sort of man', says Ramakrishna, 'who is like the pearl-oyster...The pearl-oyster leaves its bed at the bottom of the sea, and comes up to the surface to catch the rain-water when the star Svati is in the ascendant. It floats about on the surface of the sea with its shell wide open, until it has succeeded in catching a drop of the rain-water, and then it dives deep down to its sea-bed and there rests until it has succeeded in fashioning a beautiful pearl out of that rain-drop'.

A Bhakta must undergo his apprenticeship under a Guru. In a way its like swimming. If you are in your right senses, you wouldn't dream of learning to swim by jumping into a river. You would, naturally, get the help of someone experienced in the art. 'The shaping of our own destinies', says Vivekananda, 'does not preclude our receiving help from outside; nay, in the vast majority of cases, such help is absolutely necessary'.

Thus goes a Zoroastrain prayer: 'Reveal unto me a teacher who may be full of Wisdom...so innocent that the Angel of Inspiration may approach him through his loving thoughts. A true teacher is Thy beloved agent'.

The Guru may not be perfect, but we are to learn from what is worthy in him. 'Take the pearl and throw the oyster-shell away', advises Ramakrishna. 'Follow the advice given thee by the Guru and throw out of considera-tion the human frailties of thy teacher'.

But while extolling the advantages of having a Guru or 'spiritual transmitter', Vivekananda cautions us to be wary of quacks. After all, Bhakti Yoga is a little more complicated than swimming.

'There are many who, though immersed in ignorance, yet in the pride of their hearts fancy they know everything, and not only do not stop there, but offer to take others on their shoulders; and thus the blind leading the blind, both fall into the ditch...The world is full of these. Everyone wants to be a teacher, every beggar wants to make a gift of a million dollars!'

How are we to recognise a true teacher then?

Since religion is realization, 'what religion can an impure man teach?...with the teacher of religion we must first see what he is, and then what he says...what can he transmit if he has not spiritual power in himself?...The function of the teacher is indeed an affair of the transference of something, and not one of mere stimulation of the existing intellectual or other faculties in the taught'.

Also 'we must see that he knows the spirit of the scriptures. The whole world reads Bibles, Vedas, and Korans, but they are all only...the dry bones of religion. The teacher who deals too much in words, and allows the mind to be carried away by the force of words, loses the spirit ...You will find that not one of the great teachers of the world ever went into these various explanations of the texts; there is with them no attempt at 'text-torturing', no external playing upon the meaning of words and their roots. Yet they nobly taught, while others who have nothing to teach have taken up a word, sometimes, and written a three-volume book on its origin, on the man who used it first, and on what that man was accustomed to eat, and how long he slept, and so on.

'If you want to be a Bhakta, it is not at all necessary for you to know whether Krishna was born in Mathura or in Vraja, what he was doing, or just the exact date on which he pronouned the teachings of the Gita. You only require to FEEL the craving for the beautiful lessons of duty and love in the Gita.

'The third condition is in regard to the motive. The teacher must not teach with any ulterior selfish motive of money, name, or fame; his work must be simply out of love...for mankind at large'.

St. Ignatius in his book on spiritual exercises stresses the point that the retreat master should make his system flexible enough to accommodate all types of temperaments and intellects. He should not over-talk or sermonize but should, rather, help the retreants discover themselves through introspection. Vivekananda would be in complete agreement with this. The Guru should be as much a master of psychology as of spirituality. He should have the ability to accurately size up his disciple and deal with him accordingly.

I do not think Vivekananda would advise us to go out of our way in search of a Guru. When he is truly needed, he will inevitably appear: 'It is a mysterious law of nature that as soon as the field is ready the seed MUST and does come; as soon as the soul earnestly desires to have religion, the transmitter of the religious force MUST and does appear to help that soul'. It was Ramakrishna's amazing Guru, the naked Totapuri, a Yogi from Punjab who, I think, suddenly gave out one day that he must instantly leave Dakshineshwar because he could feel through his Yogic sixth sense, as it were, that somebody elsewhere was in urgent need of him!

In the preparatory stage of Bhakti Yoga, special emphasis is laid on suitable nutrition. 'The question of food has always been one of the most vital with the Bhaktas. Apart from the extravagance into which some of the Bhakti sects have run, there is a great truth underlying this question of food...The materials which we receive through our food into our body-structure go a great way to determine our mental constitution'.

Whitehead has remarked that 'it is not so widely realized that evidence is accumulating that what we eat also has a vital bearing on how we think and the general level of our intelligence'.

As we have seen, everything in nature is, for the Yogi, composed of Sattvic, Rajasic and Tamasic particles. While the adept Yogi has an extraordinary control over his senses and need not concern himself more than cursorily about such subsidiary matters, most of us would do ourselves an immense favour by paying at least as much attention to the substance of our diet as to its taste.

Ideally, there is nothing to beat good, wholesome vegetatian fare. The reason is not a moral one, seeing that plants too have life, but one pertaining to sound health. M. Gautier in a work on the subject writes that vegetarian food 'alkalizes the blood, regulates the circulation, and preserves the elasticity of the arteries...it makes one less liable to danger from maladies of the skin and the joints, and to congestions of the internal organs. It tends to soften the disposition—to make us more calm and less agitated, aggressive and violent. It is practical and rational. It ought to be accepted, if one follows an ideal for the establishment of an education for races of men who are to be sweet-tempered, intelligent, artistic, peace-loving, yet nonetheless prolific, vigorous and active'.

Cholesterol, which is indispensable to life and is mainly produced in the liver but also extracted from the food we eat, is packaged by the body in envelopes of protein. One type of cholesterol package is known as HDL or High-Density Lipoprotein. Another is LDL or Low-Density Lipoprotein. Recently, researchers have found that while HDL has a beneficial effect on health, high levels of LDL pose a potential threat to the heart. They also testify that foods of animal origin almost invariably raise LDL levels, while vegetarian diets generally tend to lower them.

People who equate vegetarianism with weakness would do well to consider the following quote from the Encyclopaedia Britannica: 'The athletic records of vegetarian schools suggest that vegetarians may excel flesh-eaters in endurance, and be excelled by them in sudden bursts of energy. Vegetarians have won international championships in such sports as running, swimming, tennis, and wrestling'.

However that may be, Vivekananda makes an earnest request to the beginner not to indulge in the 'extravagant meaningless fanaticism which has driven religion entirely to the kitchen'. Mental and spiritual foods are even more important than the food for the body, and the Bhakta should religiously cultivate the society of the holy.

To be a fit student, the Bhakta must also be strong and hardy, for the control of the organs which is essential for spiritual growth will not be possible otherwise. 'It is the strong body alone that can bear the shock of reaction resulting from the attempt to control the organs'.

'Try to gain absolute mastery over your sexual instinct', says Ramakrishna. 'If one succeeds in doing this, a physiological change is produced in the body by the development of a hitherto rudimentary nerve known by the name of Medha, whose function it is to transmute the lower energies into the higher. The knowledge of the higher self is gained after the development of this Medha nerve'.

Though trying to follow this dictum can lead to disastrous consequences for the uninitiated layman—need one elaborate on the dangers of repression?—the Bhakta's motivation and overall conditioning makes it easier for him to sublimate his sexual instinct.

As the mystic Kabir sang:

'Who has ever taught the widowed wife to burn herself
  on the pyre of her dead husband?*
And who has ever taught love to find bliss in
  renunciation?'

It is in this context that we must view Sir Andrew Clarke's observation that 'continence does not harm, it does not hinder development, it increases energy and enlivens perception'.

And Ramakrishna remarks: 'The moth once seeing the light never returns to darkness; the ant dies in the sugar-heap, but never returns therefrom. Similarly, a good devotee glady sacrifices his life for his God by renunciation'.

'The nearer we approach God', says Vivekananda, 'the more do we begin to see that all things are in Him. When the soul succeeds in appropriating the bliss of this supreme love, it also begins to see Him in everything. Our heart will thus become an eternal fountain of love. And when we

* A reference to a voluntary practice in ancient India. Thus a Greek account of the early Magadhan epoch describes the widow of an Indian commander departing to the pyre 'crowned with fillets by her women and decked out splendidly as for a wedding'. The practice stemmed from the belief, common to many primitive cultures, that life after death was a continuation of earthly life and subject to the same wants. In later times, however, it was to turn into a 'scriptural' injunction, and was declared illegal and punishable by courts only as late as 1829.

reach even higher states of this love, all the little differences between the things of the world are entirely lost; man is seen no more as man, but only as God; the animal is seen no more as animal, but as God; even the tiger is no more a tiger, but a manifestation of God'.

In his wanderings around India prior to his visit to the U.S.A., Vivekananda came across a Sadhu who was bitten by a snake. The Sadhu, who was a Bhakta, fell unconscious. When he came to, he glowed and said, 'That was a messenger from by Beloved!'

There are a few interesting sayings of Ramakrishna in this context. One goes: "Says God, 'I am the snake that biteth and the charmer that healeth; I am the judge that condemneth and the executioner that whippeth'".

This is open to misunderstanding, and Ramakrishna explains it through a parable:

"The master said, 'Everything that exists is God'. The pupil understood it literally, but not in the true spirit. While he was passing through a street, he met with an elephant. The mahut shouted aloud, 'Move away, move away!' The pupil argued in his mind, 'Why should I move away? I am God, so is the elephant also God. What fear has God of Himself?' Thinking thus he did not move. At last the elephant took him up by his trunk, and dashed him aside. He was severely hurt, and going back to his master, he related the whole adventure. The Master said, 'All right, you are God. The elephant is God also, but God in the shape of the mahut was warning you also from above. Why did you not pay heed to his warnings?'"

Vivekananda says that when the Bhakta realizes the all-pervadingness of God and reaches the state of supreme devotion, 'forms vanish, rituals fly away, books are superseded, images, churches, religions and sects, countries and nationalities—all these little limitations and bondages fall off by their own nature...' 'To him God exists entirely as love'. '...the perfected Bhakta no more goes to see God in temples and churches; he knows no place where he will not find Him. He finds Him in the temple as well as out of the temple; he finds Him in the

saint's saintliness as well as in the wicked man's wickedness, because he has Him already seated in glory in his
own heart, as the one Almighty, inextinguishable Light of
Love, which is ever shining and externally present'.

The Sufi mystic Baba Kuhi of Shiraz expresses this
feeling in a memorable verse:

In the market, in the Cloister—only God I saw.
In the valley and on the mountain—only God I saw.
Him I have seen beside me oft in tribulation;
In favour and in fortune—only God I saw.
In prayer and fasting, in praise and contemplation,
In the religion of the Prophet—only God I saw.
Neither soul nor body, accident nor substance,
Qualities nor causes—only God I saw.
I opened mine eyes and by the light of His face around
     me
In all the eye discovered—only God I saw.
Like a candle I was melting in His fire:
Amidst the flames outflanking—only God I saw.
Myself with mine eyes I saw most clearly,
But when I looked with God's eyes—only God I saw.
I passed away into nothingness, I vanished,
And lo, I was the All-living—only God I saw.

At times it has been alleged that mystical states are not
valid because they find a variety of expressions which do
not coincide in character. Only a person with a very super-
ficial acquaintance of mystical literature can arrive at such
a conclusion. Human beings are greatly varied, and likewise human relationships are various. To us God can, at
first, only assume a human form. 'We all have to begin as
dualists in the religion of love. God is to us a separate
Being, and we feel ourselves to be separate beings also.
Love then comes in the middle, and man begins to
approach God, and God also comes nearer and nearer to
man. Man takes up all the various relationships of life—as
father, as mother, as friend, as master, as lover—and
projects them on his ideal of love, on his God; and the last

point of his progress is reached when he feels that he has become absolutely merged in the object of his worship. We all begin with love for ourselves, and the unfair claims of the little self make even love selfish; at last, however, comes the full blaze of light in which this little self is seen to have become one with the Infinite. Man himself is transfigured in the presence of this Light of Love, and he realises at last the beautiful and inspiring truth that Love, the Lover and the Beloved are one'.

★★★

# Epilogue

It has been charged that 'great men' have often done more harm than good, for however much the actual worth of their wisdom, posterity has rather consistently warped it and exploited it for its own mean ends. On the face of it this analysis would appear not unreasonable. If there are men who have concerned themselves with turning base metals into gold, there are many more who have laboriously endeavoured to debase others' gold into lead. But that is not the point. When I play the 'Blue Danube' on the piano it might sound like someone is pushing heavy furniture over an uneven surface, but my personal rendition has no bearing on the merit of the composition as such. No one has the right to call Strauss names because I am not up to the mark. If mankind has not mellowed enough to plumb the eternal values of religion, the shortcoming lies not with religion but with mankind itself. It is important, as Vivekananda said, not to compromise the ideal to the real, but to lift the real to the level of the ideal. In the absence of an ideal there can be no progress, and in the absence of progress human life itself will be devoid of content. Evolution holds the promise of the advent of the Superman, and it is only a proper religion that can smooth the wheels of this process and hasten his arrival.

Like all teachings worth the name, Vivekananda's message too has suffered pollution. Stupid people, who have enjoyed a great majority everywhere at all times, always rally around the superficialities of a personality rather than his ideas. This is the indiscriminate craving for quick protection that marks out a particular species of morons. This is the beginning of deification and cult-worship, and its concomitants, enmity and strife. Vivekananda himself cried out against such propensities when he declared:

'Sectarianism, bigotry, and its horrible descendant, fanaticism, have long possessed this beautiful earth. They have filled the earth with violence, drenched it often and often with human blood, destroyed civilisations and sent whole nations to despair. Had it not been for these horrible demons, human society would be far more advanced than it is now.'

Unconsciously, and unfortunately, Vivekananda lent himself exceedingly well to the mentality of that order of people who are perpetually on the look-out for a hero whom they may place on a pedestal and worship; for here was a well-built, handsome, young celebrity with strikingly luminous eyes and a broad, high forehead and regular features and pearly-white teeth. To cap it all, he was also an intellectual! Vivekananda the sublimated sex-symbol has much more to do with these people than Vivekananda, the teacher of eternal truths! How our Swamiji would have reacted to such developments can well be imagined, for he himself never once propagated his master's message at the expense of the latter's personality. Had he done so, he once remarked, his teachings would no doubt have been far easier to sell; but their spiritual efficacy—which was what mattered—would have been correspondingly low.

Einstein is of the opinion that the cosmic religious feeling is the noblest of its kind in man. He also says that he believes in a God 'who reveals Himself in the orderly harmony of the universe. I believe that the intelligence is manifested throughout all nature'. There would have been no science, after all, if the cosmos did not possess a rational order of its own, and if men were incapable of discovering the principles underlying that order. If the findings of the mystic sages are correct—and this is something that each of us could try to verify for ourselves—then, as a systemised body of knowledge, they may well constitute a super-science, as the yogis who claim to have had a direct perception of the Truth hold they do; for the yogis seemingly use an instrument that is beyond the reach of the foremost scientists. The scientist's forte is the mind. The yogi, on the other hand, considers this too restricted for his purpose, and believes he can make use of this very mind to transcend it, just as you may stand up on a person's shoulder and be able to reach far beyond him.

Mysticism, as the quest for a hidden truth, is often dismissed as 'occult' and made to seem as an enemy of science. Yet all the 'established sciences, whether it be physics or chemistry or medicine or meteorology, were once the province of the occult, indulged in by alchemists or priests or witch doctors or shamans or others of their ilk; and it is only after they shed their exclusiveness that they ceased being occult. Parapsychology has in recent years been the focus of a great deal of attention, and terms like ESP, telepathy, clairvoyance, clairaudience and psychokinesis are increasingly making their way into the common man's vocabulary. It is an interesting conjecture whether mysticism too will not one day leave the realms of the occult, but one fact seems clear: over the long years of human history, man has gradually been expanding his field of enquiry from what is farthest outside of him to what is deepest within. From astrology, geology and physics, among the oldest of the sciences, to anthropology, sociology and psychology—three of the youngest which, even a century ago, were open to attack as spurious—the journey has been an enormous one, but the general trend of the movement has been homewards. Could mysticism—possibly under a new name once it loses its mystique—be the logical culmination to this process?

One is reminded of the story of the deer which smelled musk and searched for it everywhere and, not having found it, died in despair, never once suspecting that the musk was within itself. Man's salvation lies in the realisation that the true treasures of life are within himself.

'There is a power behind impelling us forward', says Vivekananda, 'we do not know where to seek for the real object, but this love is sending us forward in search of it. Again and again we find out our mistake. We grasp something and find it slips through our fingers and then we grip something else. Thus on and on we go, till at last comes light; we come to God...But the path to God is long and difficult.'

'Has man a future?' asks Mr Bertrand Russel, to which

Dr Arnold Toynbee replies that 'at this supremely dangerous moment in human history, the only way of salvation for mankind is an Indian way'. '...it is already becoming clear that a chapter which had a Western begining will have to have an Indian ending if it is not to end in the self-destruction of the human race'. 'The Emperor Ashoka's and the Mahatma Gandhi's principle of non-violence and Sri Ramakrishna's testimony to the harmony of religions: here we have the attitude and the spirit that can make it possible for the human race to grow together into a single family and, in the Atomic Age, this is the only alternative to destroying ourselves.

'In the Atomic Age the whole human race has an utilitarian motive for following the Indian way. No utilitarian motive could be stronger or more respectable in itself. The survival of the human race is at stake. Yet even the strongest and most respectable utilitarian motive is only a secondary reason for taking Ramakrishna's and Gandhi's and Ashoka's teaching to heart and acting on it. The primary reason is that this teaching is right—and is right because it flows from a true vision of spiritual reality.'

Political revolutions are pseudo-revolutions, revolutions from without, incapable of encompassing the entire man. You have a pain in your neck and they remove it and put it on your back and claim, 'We've healed your neck.' Quite true, of course, except that you wish they had left your back alone. And so when the ache on your back grows unbearable the cry of revolution rends the air again, and a new political ideology comes sweeping along and shifts the pain from your back to a few inches below. And so on and on it goes, but the pain, once there, then elsewhere, never ceases, because the essential you has not been touched, only the focus of your problem has changed.

We have to die to our old selves, say the mystic sages, and rise rejuvenated from its ashes to a new consciousness of oneness with our origin—the Moksa of Hinduism, the Nirvana of the Buddhists, the Unio Mystica of Western Christianity, and the Fana of Islam. That, rather than the literal interpretation it has been given in institutionalised Hinduism, is what it really means to be a 'twice-born Brahmin.' That—the evolution of consciousness and the concomitant conversion and reintegration of personality—is the ultimate revolution that leads to life:

'How can a grown man be born again?' Nicodemus asked. 'He certainly cannot enter his mother's womb and be born a second time!'

"I tell you the truth,' replied Jesus, 'that no one can enter the Kingdom of God unless he is born of water and the Spirit. Flesh gives birth to flesh, and Spirit gives birth to spirit. Do not be surprised because I tell you, 'You must all be born again.' The wind blows wherever it wishes; you hear the sound it makes, but you do not know where it comes from or where it is going. It is the same way with everyone who is born of the Spirit."

# Glossary

ARJUNA:
The hero of the epic Mahabharata; a prince who was a magnificent archer.

BHAGAVAD GITA:
The Song Divine, a metrical composition containing the sacred dialogues between Lord Krishna and Arjuna.

BOSE, J.C.:
1858-1937. A pioneer of modern Indian science who, using scientific instruments of great refinement and precision, demonstrated that plants possess life.

BOSE, SUBHAS:
Popularly known in India as 'Netaji' or 'The Revered Leader'. Freedom-fighter and spearhead of the left wing in the Indian National Congress. Having defeated Mahatma Gandhi's nominee for the party Presidency, found himself isolated and resigned to form a new party called the Forward Bloc. During the civil disobedience movement against the British, escaped from house arrest in Calcutta and reached an agreement with the Japanese. Many Indians had been taken prisoners in Singapore, Malaya, and Burma, and from their ranks Netaji organised the Indian National Army or Azad Hind Fouz, which advanced with the Japanese army to the very door-steps of India.

CHAITANYA:
1485-1533. A visionary ecstatic who founded a highly influential religious sect in eastern India and occupies a unique place of honour in medieval Bhakti history.

GHOSE,
  AUROBINDO:      1872-1950. Ages 7-14 spent in
                  England, where he received an
                  English education. Began his poli-
                  tical career on his return to India.
                  Believed that nationalism should
                  have a strong religious basis. During
                  a jail term in 1908, he underwent a
                  metamorphosis, studying the Gita
                  and practising Yoga. In 1910 he
                  retired to his hermitage in
                  Pondicherry, where he devoted the
                  rest of his life to philosophy and
                  mysticism.

KABIR:            Dates uncertain, some scholars
                  placing his birth in A.D. 1398 and
                  others in A.D. 1440. A great believer
                  in devotional worship who preached
                  a religion of love and proclaimed that
                  'the Hindus and the Mussalmans
                  have the same Lord'.

KALPA:            One whole day and night of Brahma,
                  the Creator, the first deity of the
                  Hindu trinity, amounting to
                  8640000000 years.

KRISHNA:          The eighth incarnation of Vishnu, the
                  second deity of the Hindu trinity,
                  who sustains creation; charioteer of
                  the hero Arjuna at the battlefield of
                  Kurukshetra.

RAMAKRISHNA:      1834-86. A simple temple priest at the
                  temple of goddess Kali at Dakshine-
                  shwar, four miles to the north of
                  Calcutta. A great mystic who, every
                  now and then was wont to have
                  strange fits of God-consciousness.
                  He is said to have possessed such
                  powers as seeing things at a distance,
                  healing a disease by simply willing,

and purifying a man's thoughts by merely touching his body. He learnt and practised the doctrines of all the major world faiths and arrived at the conclusion that all religions are true. His intense spirituality, and the homely simplicity and depth of his teachings attracted around him, in the later stage of his life, a dedicated band of young, educated Bengalis, among them Narendranath Datta, who was later to become the famous Swami Vivekananda. The veneration in which Vivekananda held Ramakrishna is manifest in the former's statement about the latter that 'one glance of his gracious eyes can create a hundred thousand Vivekanandas at this instant. I shall scatter his ideas broadcast over the world...'

RAMANA
MAHARSHI:    1879-1950. One of the spiritual giants of modern India, and an outstanding representative of the path of know-ledge or Jnana Yoga. The place especially associated with his name is Arunachala or Tiruvannamalai in southern India, where the sage spent fifty-four years.

RAMANUJA:    A famous religious teacher of ancient India who laid emphasis on Bhakti as a means of salvation.

ROY,
RAMMOHAN:    A towering intellectual and the father of social reform in modern India. Fought casteism and the humiliating position of women. A great champion of English education in the country,

the liberty of the Press, and the cause of the peasants. Upheld the unity of God and rejected the worship of images—on which principles he founded the Brahma Sabha in 1828. A prolific pamphleteer and publisher whose efforts gave a great boost to the development of Bengali prose.

SARASWATI,
DAYANAND:

1824-83. A Sanskrit scholar who, despite having no English education, shared many similarities with Rammohan Roy and was, like the latter, a monotheist, Founder of the great social and religious reform movement, the Arya Samaj. However, unlike Rammohan Roy, Dayanand Saraswati appealed not to an intellectual elite, but spoke directly to the masses.

SHANKARA
(CHARYA):

A Vedantist belonging to the 8th century A.D.. Considered the most powerful exponent of the doctrine of pure monism, and one of the greatest Hindu philosophers of all time.

UPANISHADS:

Secret or esoteric doctrines that comprise one of the four different classes of literary compositions in the Vedas. The Upanishads deal primarily with the concepts of Brahman and Atman—the universal or absolute soul, and the individual soul.

VEDAS:

'Veda' means knowledge. The term 'Vedas' refers to the sacred scriptures of the Hindus.

VEDANTA:

Literally, the end of the Vedas. In actual connotation, the summit of knowledge reached in the Vedas.

Vedantists lay special emphasis on the Upanishads, which to them may be said to signify what the New Testament does to Christians.

# Bibliography

(1) The Complete Works of Vivekananda: Advaita Ashrama, Calcutta.

(2) Religion And Culture by S. Radhakrishnan: Hind Pocket Books (P) Ltd.

(3) Ramakrishna: His life and Sayings by F. Max Muller: S. Gupta And Bros.

(4) Vedanta For Modern Man: Mentor

(5) Yoga, A Scientific Evaluation by Kovoor T. Behanan: Martin Secker And Warburg Ltd., London

(6) Enstein—My Views: Ganesh And Co., Madras.

(7) Mysticism, A Study And Anthology by F.C. Happold: Penguin

(8) Japasutram, The Science of Creative Sound by Swami Pratyagatmananda Saraswati, with intros. by Charu Chandra Chatterji and Justice P.B. Mukharji

(9) Poems of Kabir, translated by Rabindranath Tagore: Macmillan And Co.

(10) Infinite Bliss by I.J. Singh: Narankari Printing Press, New Delhi

(11) Horizon, Winter 1974, Vol. XVI, No. 1: The Cosmos Is A Giant Thought by Robert Hughes

(12) How to Know God: The Yoga Aphorisms Of Patanjali, translated with a new commentary by Swami Prabhavananda and Christopher Isherwood: George Allen And Unwin Ltd.

(13) The Life Of Vivekananda And The Universal Gospel by Romain Rolland: Advaita Ashrama, Calcutta

(14) Adventures in Religious Life by Swami Yatiswarananda: Sri Ramkrishna Math, Mylapore, Madras

(15) Vedanta And The Social Philosophy Of Swami Vivekananda: Santwana Dasgupta

(16) Psychic Discoveries Behind The Iron Curtain by Sheila Ostrander and Lynn Schroeder: Bantam Books

(17) Real Magic by Philip Bonewits: Sphere Books Ltd., London

(18) The Book On The Taboo Against Knowing Who You Are by Alan Watts: Sphere Books Ltd.

(19) The Tibetan Book Of The Dead: Compiled and edited by W.Y. Evans-Wentz: Oxford University Press

(20) A Guide For The Perplexed by E.F. Schumacher: Jonathan Cape

(21) The New Encyclopaedia Britannica

(22) The Five Great Religions by Edward Rice: Bantam Books

(23) Reincarnation: The Second Chance by Sybil Leek (Bantam Books, New York)

★★★